SEMINAR STUDIES IN HISTORY

General Editor: Roger Lockyer

Bismarck and Germany, 1862–1890

D. G. Williamson

Head of History and Politics
Highgate School, London

LONGMAN
London and New York

LONGMAN GROUP UK LIMITED
Longman House, Burnt Mill, Harlow, Essex CM20 2JI
and Associated Companies throughout the world
Published in the United States of America
by Longman Inc., New York.

First published 1986
Eighth impression 1994

ISBN 0 582 35413 7

Set in 10/11 Linotron Baskerville

Printed in Malaysia by VP

The publisher's policy is to use paper manufactured from sustainable forests.

For A. M. W.

British Library Cataloguing in Publication Data
Williamson, D. G.
  Bismarck and Germany, 1862–1890. – (Seminar
  studies in history)
  1. Bismarck, Otto, *Fürst von* 2. Germany –
  Politics and government – 1848–1870 3. Germany
  – Politics and government – 1871–1918
  I. Title II. Series
  943.08'092'4   DD218
  ISBN 0-582-35413-7

Library of Congress Cataloging in Publication Data
Williamson, D. G.
  Bismarck and Germany, 1862–1890.
  (Seminar studies in history)
  Bibliography: p.
  Includes index.
  1. Germany – History – 1871–1918. 2. Germany –
History – 1848–1870. 3. Bismarck, Otto, Fürst von,
1815–1898. I. Title. II. Series.
  DD220.W48 1986 943.08 85-19714
  ISBN 0-582-35413-7

Contents

Contents

Acknowledgements

We are grateful to the following for permission to reproduce copy-right material:
George Allen & Unwin Ltd for extracts from pp. 104, 148, 221, 226 *Germany in the Age of Bismarck* Ed. W. M. Simon; Harper & Row Inc. for extracts from pp. 142–3, 180–2, 186–7 *The Age of Bismarck, Documents and Interpretation* (1973) Ed. T. S. Hamerow; the author, Professor W. N. Medlicott, for extracts from pp. 21, 30–1, 48–9, 128–9, 142 *Bismarck and Europe* Ed. Medlicott & Coveney; the editor, *Past and Present*, and the author, Professor Hans Ulrich Wehler, for an extract from his article 'Bismarck Imperialism, 1862–1890' pp. 122–3 *Past and Present* No. 48 (Aug. 1970); Franz Steiner Verlag for extracts and Table from *Free Trade Protection in Germany* by I. N. Lambi, © Franz Steiner Verlag 1963, formerly Wiesbaden, now Stuttgart, W. Germany; University of Nebraska for extracts from pp. 149, 106–7 *The Social and Political Conflict in Prussia 1858–64* by Eugene N. Anderson, Copyright 1954 by The University of Nebraska.
Cover: "The Visionary", portrait of Otto von Bismarck by B. Schmidhammer from *Jugend*, 1908. Photo: Mary Evans Picture Library.

Seminar Studies in History
Founding Editor: Patrick Richardson

Introduction

The Seminar Studies series was conceived by Patrick Richardson, whose experience of teaching history persuaded him of the need for something more substantial than a textbook chapter but less formidable than the specialised full-length academic work. He was also convinced that such studies, although limited in length, should provide an up-to-date and authoritative introduction to the topic under discussion as well as a selection of relevant documents and a comprehensive bibliography.

Patrick Richardson died in 1979, but by that time the Seminar Studies series was firmly established, and it continues to fulfil the role he intended for it. This book, like others in the series, is therefore a living tribute to a gifted and original teacher.

Note on the System of References:
A bold number in round brackets (**5**) in the text refers the reader to the corresponding entry in the Bibliography section at the end of the book. A bold number in square brackets, preceded by 'doc.' [**doc. 6**] refers the reader to the corresponding item in the section of Documents, which follows the main text.

ROGER LOCKYER
General Editor

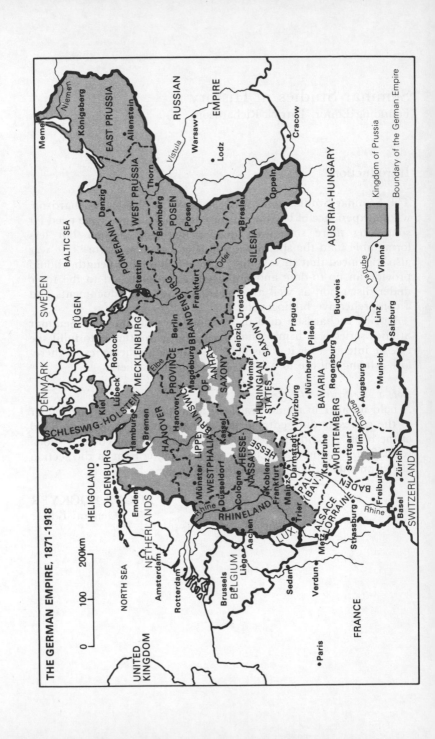

THE GERMAN EMPIRE, 1871-1918

Kingdom of Prussia

Boundary of the German Empire

Part One: The Setting

1 The Background

Most German historians up to 1945 – with the notable exception of Eckart Kehr, whose pioneering studies in the late twenties on such novel themes as the influence of economic interest groups on Wilhelmine armament policy make him the 'father of German historical revisionism' (**79** Introd.) [**doc. 1**] – were apt to dismiss a consideration of the role of anything but diplomatic and military history in the unification of Germany as 'unheroic and bourgeois' (**94** p. 331). Today, however, the tendency, even among non-Marxist historians, is to concentrate more on the inter-relationship between diplomatic, social and economic factors. Bismarck did not fashion German unity alone. He exploited powerful forces which already existed: the industrial revolution in Germany, the growth of liberalism and nationalism [**doc. 2**], the disintegration of the 1815 Vienna settlement during and after the Crimean War, and the increasing determination of Prussia after 1848 to reassert her influence over Germany (**40**).

The rapid industrialisation of the German states between 1850 and 1870 removed a number of economic and geographical barriers to unification. The growth of industry and the construction of railways were decisive factors in uniting the far-flung provinces of Prussia and in enabling her to assert her power more effectively within Germany. Thanks to her possession of the Ruhr and Silesia, Prussia developed an overwhelming lead in the production of coal and iron which inevitably gave her a commanding economic position within Germany. The growth of the railways, the banking system and above all the development of the *Zollverein** increased the mutual economic interdependence of the German states and so created a complex internal trading pattern. This arguably made economic unity a reality a decade or so before political unity was achieved (**94**), although the great commercial ports of Hamburg and Bremen remained outside the *Zollverein* until the 1880s.

Understandably reacting to the excessive emphasis on military

---

* Words marked with asterisk are explained in the glossary.

and diplomatic history, some historians have exaggerated the role of the German Customs Union or *Zollverein* in the unification of Germany, and have seen the 'establishment of the Empire of 1871 as merely the formal completion of a unity already achieved in the economic sphere' (**77** p. 340). The creation of the *Zollverein* in 1834 was initially an economic measure which aimed to free inter-German trade so that Prussia, with her lengthy frontiers, would not be committed to maintaining expensive and ineffective customs posts (**72**). Nevertheless the political implications of the *Zollverein* soon emerged.

In 1815 the creation of the German Confederation under the presidency of Austria gave Vienna a decisive position in German affairs. The *Zollverein*, however, was the one sphere in pan-German politics from which Austria was excluded. After 1848 Prussia systematically blocked all Austrian attempts to enter the *Zollverein*. In 1852 she skilfully deferred negotiations for a joint Austro-German customs union until 1860. In 1862 Prussian enthusiasm for a free-trade agreement between France and the *Zollverein* was again politically motivated. It was an effective means for permanently excluding Austria, as her industry was too weak to face open competition with France within the *Zollverein* (**71, 77**).

Few would dispute that the *Zollverein* was a powerful factor in the eventual exclusion of Austria from a Prussian dominated *Kleindeutschland**, but it is by no means clear that it could have achieved German unity unaided by other factors. The lesser German states clung tenaciously to their independence, which was guaranteed by the rule that decisions within the *Zollverein* could only be taken unanimously, and suspiciously blocked any attempts by Prussia to streamline the voting procedure. In 1866 the South German states were not deterred by their membership of the *Zollverein* from allying with Austria against Prussia. Arguably, close economic links had made 'scarcely a dent in the traditional political hostility' (**67** p. 294).

An important consequence of Prussia's economic policy was that the Berlin government could count on increasing backing from the *Kleindeutsch* Liberals in the German states (**68, 76 Vol. 2**) [**doc. 2**]. Within a decade of their defeat in 1848 the Liberals had again become a powerful political and social force throughout Germany and in the Prussian elections of 1858 they gained an overwhelming majority. The defeat of Austria by Napoleon III and the triumph of nationalism in Italy in 1859–60 gave still greater impetus to the *Kleindeutsch* cause and led to the foundation of the *Nationalverein** [**docs. 3, 4**]. By co-ordinating the policies of the *Kleindeutsch* Liberals in each state, this attempted to exert pressure on the German rulers to work towards the creation of a unified Germany under the Prussian crown (**68**).

When Prince William of Prussia became Regent in 1858, both the Crown and the Liberal majority in the *Landtag** shared the same explicit aim of unifying Germany under Prussian leadership. He had welcomed the Radowitz Plan in 1849 for a union of the German states under the Prussian Crown, which he authorised his foreign minister von Bernstorff to revive in 1861 – an initiative which Pflanze sees as marking the commencement of 'a drama whose denouement was to be on the battlefields of Bohemia in 1866' (**30** p. 152).

However, just at the moment when the interests of the Liberal majority and of the Prussian Crown seemed to coincide, a major constitutional crisis arose which threatened to ruin the great opportunities in foreign policy afforded Prussia by the very favourable European diplomatic situation (**121**). William, horrified at the inefficiencies revealed in the organisation and performance of the Prussian army during the mobilisation of 1859, was determined both to increase and drastically to restructure the army. In 1860 the Minister of War, von Roon, put before the *Landtag* a comprehensive scheme which practically doubled the size of the field army, increased the period of conscription to three years and separated the militia from the front-line units (**30, 95**).

Although it is true that both sides 'muddled into conflict' (**68** p. 101) and that a compromise on details was often possible, nevertheless the army bill did raise an important issue – namely the position of the army in a constitutional state (**99**). Downgrading the militia into a 'home guard' threatened the fundamental Liberal conception of a civilianised army, which dated from 1814–15 and was 'as important to the Liberals as . . . the rights of man' (**30** p. 160). William, who became King in 1861, ultimately refused to compromise because he wished to restore undiluted the hereditary power of the Crown over the armed forces, and to purge the operational army of civilian elements which might undermine the traditional loyalties of the army to the Crown [**doc. 5**]. As late as 1934 one German historian described the constitutional crisis as 'the central event in the domestic history of Germany in the last hundred years' (**95** p. 137).

The real break between King and Parliament did not occur until March 1862. At first the moderate, or 'Old Liberal', majority, despite rejecting key clauses in the army bill, twice granted provisional appropriations to cover the initial cost of military expansion. It was even prepared to abandon the militia, but the Crown rejected any compromise and proceeded with the full implementation of the bill. Consequently within the Liberal movement opinion polarised and the more radical German Progressive Party was formed, which in the elections of December 1861 became the largest party in the *Landtag*. In March 1862 the *Landtag* ensured a confrontation with the Crown by approving the Hagen proposal, which, by demanding a full breakdown of the figures in the military budget, attempted to make unconstitutional government efforts to manipulate funds, unauthorised by Parliament. William replied by dissolving the *Landtag*, but he failed to conjure up a Conservative majority in the subsequent elections. His consistent refusal to accept the modest compromise put forward by his own Cabinet caused the resignation of two senior ministers, Heydt and Bernstorff, which even his threat to abdicate could not prevent. It was then that he appointed Bismarck to lead a crisis cabinet specifically pledged to implement the army bill.

2 The Bismarck Debate

Despite the current tendency to concentrate on the socio-economic background to German unification, it is impossible to avoid the towering figure of Bismarck. The number of studies on Bismarck has reached truly 'staggering proportions' (**30** p. 3). In 1966 it was calculated that there were over 6,000 books and articles on him (**29**), many of which, particularly those written before 1945, are laudatory almost to the point of hagiography.

The experiences of the Nazi period encouraged historians to re-appraise Bismarck's achievements and to ask, like Meinecke writing in the shadow of 1945, 'whether the germs of the later evil were not already present in the Bismarckian *Reich*' (**146** p. 13). With the notable exception of Eyck (**24**), however, whose monumental Bismarck biography was published in Switzerland during the Second World War, most German historians (**149, 155**) up to the early 1960s agreed with Kaehler that any attempt to link Bismarck with Hitler was 'legend', 'prejudice' and 'propaganda' (**30** p. 4). Many foreign historians on the other hand were quicker to see a direct causal link between the Bismarck era and the horrors of the Third *Reich*. The American historian, Otto Pflanze, whose authoritative study of the unification of Germany (**30**) is still unequalled, argued, for example, that 'if one line of development runs from the revolution of 1848 through Treitschke to Hitler another certainly goes from Bismarck through Ludendorff to Hitler' (**155** p. 566).

It was Fritz Fischer's seminal study of Germany's aims in the 1914–18 war (**145**) and the emergence of the new, predominantly left-wing, post-war generation of German historians in the sixties which paved the way for a radical re-appraisal of the political and social structure of the Second *Reich* (**73**). By the mid-seventies, as a result of the re-publication of Kehr's essays (**79**) and important new works by Boehme, Wehler and Stürmer (**49, 63, 64, 71, 140, 141**), the traditional interpretations of Bismarck had been replaced by what Professor Sheehan called a 'new orthodoxy' (**73** p. 16) [**doc. 6**]. This roundly condemned Bismarck 'for perpetuating the

5

political nonage of the German people by buttressing the sagging position of the militarist *Junker** class and by emasculating Germany's parliament' (**144** p. 306). Imperial Germany is characterised as an unstable, plebiscitary dictatorship comparable to the French Second Empire, in which the military and agrarian elites retained their position through a mixture of overt repression, skilful manipulation of the political parties, 'social imperialism' (the opportune diversion of demands for political reform into enthusiasm for foreign conquest), and negative integration whereby certain groups were branded as *Reichsfeinde** to encourage a general coalition (*Sammlung**) of the forces of the right (**57, 73**).

The very comprehensiveness of this interpretation, however, is beginning to be challenged. One scholar has recently criticised Professor Stürmer (**159**) for taking too much satisfaction 'in counting the warts on Bismarck's countenance' (**157** p. 368). Another (**57** p. 195) has questioned the applicability of the Bonapartist model to Bismarck, arguing that 'there is nothing exclusively or quintessentially Bonapartist about cajoling, deceiving or throttling one's constituents'. Meanwhile, detailed research by English historians is beginning to suggest that the 'new orthodoxy' underestimates the grass-roots pressure exerted on Bismarck and the German elites and misleadingly depicts the German Empire 'as a puppet theatre with *Junkers* and industrialists pulling the strings and the middle and the lower classes dancing jerkily across the stage of history towards the final curtain of the III *Reich*' (**73** p. 23).

3 Bismarck, 1815–62

Bismarck was born in 1815 into an old Junker family in Branden-
burg, but thanks to the influence of his mother, Wilhelmina
Mencken, who descended from a distinguished but bourgeois
family of civil servants and academics and whose father had been
secretary of the royal cabinet, he was a frequent visitor to the Prussian royal household. Yet until 1847 he remained a brilliant
misfit. He only began to acquire a public reputation when he
became a deputy in the Prussian United Diet in 1847 (**22, 25, 26,
29, 30**). Bismarck's spirited and die-hard defence of the old order
in 1848 in the aftermath of the revolts won him considerable influence behind the scenes when royal power was re-established in
November (**29**). His loyalty was awarded by his appointment to
the key post of Prussian representative at the revived Federal Diet
at Frankfurt. He appeared to be the ideal man for co-operating with
the Austrians, for he had vigorously defended the orthodoxy of the
1815 settlement and opposed any concession to Liberalism or
German Nationalism, including Radowitz's half-hearted plan for a
union of German princes under the Prussian Crown. He was one
of the few Prussian Conservatives to welcome the Olmütz agreement which restored the German Confederation in 1850.

Within a fortnight of his appointment Bismarck had, however,
become highly critical of Austrian foreign policy (**24**). He undoubt-
edly took personal offence at the arrogance of the Austrian delegate
(**32**), but there were also fundamental differences between the two
powers, which no shared conservative ideology could bridge.
Austria's suspicions of Prussian policy had been reawakened by the
Radowitz plan and consequently after Olmütz, Schwarzenberg, the
Austrian Prime Minister, did not revert to the policy of close co-
operation which had been pursued by Metternich prior to 1848. He
sought to assert Austrian primacy over Prussia. Bismarck countered by advising his government to take every opportunity to seize
the leadership of Germany. He was ready 'to consider all possible
means to that end' (**30** p. 124) [**doc. 7**].

Bismarck played a major rôle in blocking Austrian membership of the *Zollverein* (**32**). When the Crimean War broke out in 1854, he urged his government to exploit Austria's rift with Russia, caused by her benevolent neutrality towards Britain and France. The war created a lasting estrangement between Vienna and St. Petersburg. The subsequent Treaty of Paris destroyed both Russia's ability and will to maintain the Vienna Settlement in Central Europe. Russian diplomacy was now directed towards abrogating the Black Sea clauses of the Treaty and consequently created a more fluid international situation, which Bismarck in a series of brilliant memoranda urged Berlin to exploit. In 1856–7 he argued that Prussia occupied a 'pivotal position' (**30**, p. 103) between the two revisionist powers, Russia and France on the one side and Britain and Austria on the other. Consequently he argued that Prussia should use it to extract concessions. In March 1858 he recommended for the first time the revolutionary step of harnessing the power of German nationalism as a means of destroying Austrian influence within Germany [**doc. 8**].

Bismarck's Machiavellian proposals were not acted upon in Berlin. When Prince William became Regent in 1857, he sent Bismarck first to St. Petersburg and then to Paris as Prussian ambassador, where Bismarck continued to pen a stream of far-sighted and radical memoranda on Prussian foreign policy. However, it was not these that secured Bismarck the post of Prime Minister of Prussia in September 1862 but rather the King's urgent need for a strong man to defy Parliament. Von Roon managed to persuade the King that Bismarck, though he toyed with German nationalism and advocated a French alliance, was just such a man.

Part Two: The Defeat of Austria

4 The Constitutional Conflict and the Liberal Opposition

Bismarck's achievements are so dazzling that historians have understandably tended to reconstruct a 'marvellous march of events, in which each stage seems to slip into its pre-appointed place' (**26**, p. 128). In fact Bismarck was faced with almost insuperable problems in both domestic and foreign policy during the years 1862–66 and he could only feel his way to solutions, keeping as many options as possible open. To understand these years it is wise to heed Stern's warning not 'to see his life backwards, beginning as it were with his success. For this perspective slights his years of struggle when he was groping his way to solutions' (**93**, p. 23).

The day after Bismarck was appointed Prime Minister, the *Landtag* escalated the constitutional crisis by striking out of the 1862 budget the funds which the Government had already earmarked for the army. Bismarck was torn between hoping to solve the constitutional conflict before it fatally impaired his freedom of action in foreign policy (**30**), and prolonging it so that he would continue to be indispensable to the King (**32**). His initial reaction was to seek a compromise, but his room for manoeuvre was severely restricted by the King's absolute refusal to amend the army bill [**doc. 5**] and by the knowledge that if he showed himself too conciliatory, he would be replaced by Manteuffel, the Chief of the Military Cabinet. Manteuffel regarded Bismarck as an unreliable maverick and he openly advocated a return to absolutism (**95**).

Bismarck's initial steps were conciliatory. He established contact with the moderate wing of the Progressive Liberals, withdrew the budget bill for 1863[1] and at his first session with the Budget Committee of the *Landtag* made, in the notorious 'blood and iron speech' [**doc. 9**], a crudely phrased attempt to unite Parliament on the basis of a revisionist foreign policy. Bismarck had intended to be conciliatory, but with his 'dangerous gift of framing pregnant and pithy sentences' (**27**, p. 166) he succeeded only in polarising

---

[1] First presented in May 1862. There were thus two budgets before the *Landtag*.

opinions still further. Behind the scenes, Roon, almost certainly with Bismarck's support, drafted a new army bill, which aimed to split the Liberal opposition by going some way towards their demand for a reduction in the length of military service. Possibly it might have won some support in the *Landtag*, but even this concession was rejected by the King despite the fact that Roon in no way conceded parliamentary control over the army.

Bismarck skilfully avoided a direct confrontation with the *Landtag* by leaving the Lords to reject the amendments to the 1862 budget bill. When the Liberals protested, the *Landtag* was prorogued. To justify the unauthorised expenditure on military reorganisation Bismarck argued that the deadlock between the two houses of Parliament created a 'constitutional hiatus' (**30**, p. 194), which the government had a duty to fill. Bismarck's interpretation, however opportune, was legally and constitutionally defensible. Unless the Liberals were ready to take to the streets or to stage a tax strike, they were powerless to challenge it, as the constitution contained no provisions for the resolution of such a crisis.

When Parliament re-assembled in January 1863 relations between Bismarck and the opposition deteriorated still further. For the next six months at least Bismarck was involved 'in a desperate fight for political survival' (**25**, p. 282). Not only did the deadlock over the budget remain unbroken, but Bismarck made a serious error of judgement in negotiating the *Alvensleben* convention with Russia, which provided for common action in suppressing a revolt in Russian Poland. The convention incensed the Liberals, alienated Britain and France, and shook the King's still somewhat fragile confidence in Bismarck, so that for a time his dismisal was seriously considered (**93**). Bismarck could only effectively defend himself by convincing the King of his indispensability. Consequently, until the *Landtag* was prorogued in May, Bismarck lost no opportunity of stressing his loyalty to the Crown and provoking the *Landtag* into fresh attacks on the King's Government. Indeed it is arguable that he deliberately tried to complicate the domestic situation (**32, 93**).

By late summer 1863 Bismarck had established, with the full-hearted support of the Crown, a degree of governmental control in Prussia that barely stopped short of a dictatorship. The Civil Service was disciplined and Liberal officials were subjected to uncomfortable reprisals for their political opinions. The Press Edict of 1 June, which was based on a similar law issued by Napoleon III, effectively stopped discussion of internal political matters by the Liberal press, and a further decree banned the discussion of politically sensitive matters by municipal councils. By the standards of the time Bismarck's measures were both arbitrary and severe, but they failed to prevent another large Liberal majority in the general election of October 1863.

Over the next three years Bismarck considered the possibility of a *coup d'état* on the French pattern of 1851. Like many nineteenth-century statesmen who had come into conflict with the Liberal middle classes, he was impressed by the way Napoleon III had exploited universal franchise to win mass support for an autocratic regime. In the summer of 1863 informed sources were convinced that Bismarck was trying to persuade the King to agree to a *coup d'état*. (**93**). Certainly in May Bismarck started a series of exploratory discussions with Ferdinand Lassalle, the leader of the newly created General Workers Union. Both were interested for their own reasons in destroying Liberalism. Simultaneously Bismarck also prodded his reluctant Cabinet into considering schemes for social reform, so that if necessary he would be able to draw up a programme designed to attract a mass electorate. Bismarck did, however, decide to play for time and keep his options open. Unless a sudden acute crisis occurred, Bismarck's inclination was to draw out the crisis until support for the Liberals waned (**30**). In June 1865, after the Diet had consistently refused funds to pay for the Danish war, a *coup d'état* was again discussed in the Prussian Crown Council, but Bismarck advised that a final decision should be deferred until the new year when the *Landtag* was due to meet.

The Liberal opposition was in reality a paper tiger, despite its imposing parliamentary majority. The government controlled the bureaucracy, was confident of the loyalty of the army, and above all was able to collect taxes from a population that was growing steadily richer. Bismarck was indeed fortunate to come to power 'during an upswing of the business cycle' (**68**, p. 441). The opposition was composed of an unstable coalition between the Old Liberals, the Left Centre and the Progressives. Each of these groups lacked internal cohesion and a secure extra-parliamentary base.

There is considerable debate about the degree of public support in Prussia for the Liberals. While it is true that the Liberals won an impressive number of elections between 1857 and 1863, the Prussian three-class voting system, by discriminating against the peasantry and the working classes, effectively ensured that the majority of the Liberals' votes came from the middle classes. Consequently it is hard to prove that Prussia 'was actually or potentially – and to an overwhelming extent – in favour of liberal reform' (**68**, p. 440). More recent studies (**30, 66**) on the contrary have argued that the Liberals had no mass backing and stress that they were fundamentally a middle-class party. The great majority of the Liberals did not desire to subject the government to complete parliamentary control, nor did they want to introduce universal franchise. It is thus not surprising that the Liberals frequently displayed 'the uncertainty of front-line troops thinly deployed before a determined foe and backed by no reserves' (**30**, pp. 181–2).

While the constitutional conflict drove Bismarck and the Liberal opposition further apart, paradoxically he achieved results in his economic and foreign policy which '*de facto* realised the programme of *Kleindeutsch* Liberalism' (**25**, p. 271). Bismarck did not share the contemporary Conservative view that the small independent artisan should be defended against the encroaching powers of modern capitalism. Although he did not move nearly as quickly as the Liberals would have liked, the whole drift of his economic policy was towards creating a climate favourable to the development of laissez-faire capitalism (**71, 76 Vol. 2**). The Mining Law of 24 June 1865, for example, which established freedom of exploration and exploitation, met with universal approval from the various chambers of commerce [**doc. 10**]. His main achievement was energetically to continue the exclusion of Austria from the *Zollverein* and, through a series of free-trade agreements with Belgium, England, Italy and France, to ensure the integration of the Prussian economy in the free-trade system of western Europe (**71**). Inevitably Bismarck's economic policy created an area of consensus between the Government and the Liberals, which facilitated an eventual constitutional settlement after Königgratz. It also convinced powerful and influential bankers like Bleichröder and Hausemann that Bismarck's foreign policy was worth financing (**93**).

The obvious success of Bismarck's foreign policy after 1864 also began to undermine the strength of the opposition. To many contemporaries it seemed that Bismarck was attempting to divert attention from the domestic crisis by the classic recipe of seeking adventures abroad. Publicly Bismarck insisted on the primacy of foreign policy over domestic policy, and until recently most German historians have accepted this at face value. Ritter, for example, is emphatic that Bismarck risked war 'only in the "innermost" interests of his country' (**99**, p. 246). More recent research has, however, re-emphasised that 'the relation between domestic

conflict and foreign aggression was close and complex' (**93**, p. 69).
It is undeniable that Bismarck had laid down the main aims of his
foreign policy before he took office, but as the constitutional conflict
deepened he increasingly appreciated that a decisive victory over
Austria would, as a by-product, enable him to make his peace with
the Liberals, although an equally decisive check would have led to
the termination of his career.

It was the Schleswig-Holstein crisis which first seriously began
to divide the Liberals. They were, as Bismarck had intended (**95**),
impressed by the Prussian victory at Düppel [**doc. 11**] in April
1864. As it became clear in the course of the following twelve
months that Bismarck was manoeuvring to annex the duchies
outright, the Liberals were confronted with an agonising dilemma
as to whether they should support a national policy or stand fast
over the constitutional conflict (**30, 66**). The old Liberals were won
over to Bismarck's policy, but the Left-Centre and Progressives
were so deeply split that they were hardly capable of active opposition during the 1865 session of the *Landtag*.

Despite their disarray a compromise solution to the constitutional conflict was still hard to achieve. In January 1865
Bismarck and Roon had once again tried to persuade the King to
compromise, but William, preferring Manteuffel's advice, cate-
gorically refused to tinker with the army bill (**95**). Bismarck was
forced, therefore, to repeat his tactics of the spring of 1863, and in
the 1865 and early 1866 sessions of the *Landtag* he once again
protected his own position by vigorously defending the Crown and
mounting a vehement attack on the opposition. This culminated
in the prosecution of two Progressive deputies for making speeches
critical of the Government on the floor of the *Landtag*, and in the
seizure of parliamentary papers and documents after the *Landtag*
had been prorogued. Through such tactics as these Bismarck, by
the spring of 1866, had merely succeeded in reuniting the fragmented
opposition at the very moment when war with Austria was imminent. The growing consensus between Bismarck and the Liberals
on foreign and economic policy appeared to vanish, and by May
1866, despite his open championship of German nationalism and
belated attempts to win over individual Liberals, 'the predominant
"movement" among the German people . . . was anti-war and anti-
Bismarck' (**30**, p. 321) [**doc. 12**].

Once the war started, however, the traditional alchemy of patriotism began to work and public opinion rapidly veered round to
supporting Bismarck. The elections for the *Landtag*, which had been

dissolved on 9 May 1866, were held whilst Prussian troops were advancing into Bohemia. Predictably the Liberals suffered a severe defeat, losing 142 seats to the Conservatives. The decisive victory of Königgratz finally secured Bismarck's position. It enabled him subsequently to settle the constitutional conflict and reconstruct the political and diplomatic map of North Germany. In retrospect 'the marvellous march of events' (**26**, p. 128) assumes an air of inevitability. Yet had Austria won the war or even forced a prolonged conflict, which would have given time for war-weariness to affect Prussia, Bismarck might have been forced to resign or even have been impeached.

5 The Road to Königgratz

Bismarck was a diplomat of genius, but even he would have failed if his policy had provoked large scale opposition from the great powers. It is a truism that Bismarck's 'skill alone is insufficient to explain the absence of hostile coalitions' (**121**, p. 3). An essential pre-condition of Austrian defeat in Germany was the collapse in the Crimean War of the Austro-Russian axis which had been instrumental in defeating the Hungarian revolt in 1849 and in subsequently re-asserting Austrian influence in Germany (**126**). Any regrouping of the powers to preserve the *status quo* in Germany was further impeded by almost universal mistrust of Napoleon III. French annexation of Nice and Savoy in 1860 renewed British suspicion of Bonapartism, whilst French support for Italian claims to Venetia prevented any early Franco-Austrian rapprochement. Napoleon's call for a European congress to solve the Polish problem in 1863 similarly terminated any immediate prospect of Franco-Russian co-operation. Both Britain and Russia were to welcome German unification as a potential check on France, and each regarded Germany as a possible ally against the other.

Bismarck has been criticised for attempting to force European diplomacy into a preconceived mould during his first few months in power. One historian has argued that 'the most striking features of Bismarck's first year as Prime Minister were the irrelevance of most of his actions [and] his apparent lack of understanding of the real forces at work in Prussia, in Germany [and] in Europe' (**22**, p. 144). Bismarck, however, inherited a situation which vindicated his long-standing suspicion of Austrian intentions. Ever since 1852 Bismarck had analysed European diplomacy in terms of Austro-Prussian rivalry and had consistently argued that Austrian domination of Germany could only be broken with French or Russian assistance.

As the *Zollverein* treaties were due for renewal in 1865, the struggle for the economic supremacy of Germany was entering its decisive stage (**77**). Berlin was determined to engineer the permanent exclusion of Austria from the *Zollverein* by negotiating a free-trade treaty with France. This, it was hoped, would form the basis of the reconstituted *Zollverein* in 1865 and so effectively pre-empt Austrian membership, since her economy was too weak to face French competition. Vienna failed to prevent the signature of the treaty but retaliated by attempting to strengthen her position within the Confederation by a subtle programme of gradual reforms (**114**).

In the autumn of 1862 Bismarck lost little time in sounding out the French and bluntly warning the Austrians of his intention to establish Prussian hegemony in North Germany. However his confident assumption of French support was shaken when Napoleon both refused to commit himself in advance to benevolent neutrality and also rejected his request that all negotiations on free-trade treaties between France and the other German states should be conducted solely through the medium of Berlin. Bismarck had hoped that this would strengthen Prussia's hands in the *Zollverein* negotiations and enable him to compel the smaller states to accept a reformed customs union with its own Prussian-dominated parliament. To avoid complete isolation Bismarck hastily changed course and offered Austria the option of a conservative alliance which would have guaranteed Austrian interests in Italy and the Near East whilst conceding Prussian hegemony in North Germany. Austria, however, persisted with her proposals for the reform of the Confederation, which were only defeated by a small majority in the Federal Diet on 22 January after intense Prussian lobbying. If Bismarck had failed he would have had little option but to appeal to *Kleindeutsch* German nationalism. Had this happened the war of 1866 might well have occurred in 1863 (**114**).

Bismarck's pursuit of the French alliance was a logical and defensible policy, if rather clumsily executed, but he made a serious error when he over-reacted to the revolt in Russian Poland in January 1863. He authorised General von Alvensleben to negotiate with the Russians a draft convention providing for military action against Polish rebels who crossed into Prussian Poland. Traditionally the convention has been hailed as a far-sighted move to secure Russian support (**24**), but at the time the reaction it caused in London, Paris and Vienna threatened to isolate Prussia and threw Bismarck on the defensive. He immediately disowned the convention and proposed to Vienna and St. Petersburg a revival of the Holy Alliance. Austria, however, resumed the initiative for Confederate reform and in August the Emperor personally invited William to a specially convened congress of princes in an attempt to by-pass Bismarck. Only after hours of passionate argument was Bismarck able to dissuade the King from attending.

Further Austrian initiatives were discouraged by Napoleon's sudden call for a European congress to revise the settlement of 1815 and by the increasingly threatening situation in Schleswig-Holstein (**124**). Ever since 1848 Schleswig-Holstein had been a *cause célèbre* of German nationalism' (**24**, p. 233). The duchies were autonomous but under the sovereignty of the King of Denmark. Holstein was predominantly German and a member of the German Confederation, whereas Schleswig, with its mixed German and Danish population, was not, although the Germans insisted that historically both duchies were inseparable. In 1848 the Danish government had attempted to absorb Schleswig into Denmark, but an immediate revolt by the German population moved the Frankfurt Parliament to authorise Prussian military intervention. This was, however, speedily halted by Anglo-Russian diplomatic pressure. In 1852 the Treaty of London was signed by the great powers, including Austria and Prussia, but it failed to solve the problem. Whilst declaring that Denmark and the duchies should be united into 'one well-ordered whole' (**24**, p. 80), it also stipulated that Schleswig should never be incorporated into Denmark. Over the next decade relations between the Germans and the Dancs deteriorated, a process only accelerated by the growth in German nationalism. In March 1863 Frederick VII, emboldened by Swedish support and growing Austro-Prussian tension, created a unitary constitution for Schleswig and Denmark. The German Confederation reacted slowly and cumbrously, but, urged on by both *Klein-* and *Grossdeutsch** nationalists, it demanded the repeal of the new constitution. The crisis was heightened by the unexpected death of Frederick. Despite the provisions of the London Treaty in favour of a Danish prince, this enabled the German pretender to the duchies, Frederick of Augustenburg, to proclaim himself Duke of Schleswig-Holstein, to the delight of German nationalists who rallied to his support throughout Germany.

Bismarck had consistently advocated that, unless Prussia could annex the territories outright, Danish sovereignty was preferable to their independence under a German ruler who would probably oppose Prussian interests in the Confederation and *Zollverein* [**doc. 13**]. He was aware of their strategic importance and in November 1862 ordered the Prussian army to draw up plans for an invasion of Schleswig-Holstein. A year later such plans seemed academic. Not only was the *status quo* guaranteed by the great powers, but increasing Confederate involvement threatened to prevent independent Prussian action. Bismarck's studied moderation in the autumn of 1863 can be attributed to the need to convince the powers of Prussia's essential willingness to observe the Treaty of London. In October 1863 he considered the possibility of British mediation and in November he began to work with the Austrians in order to prevent the Confederation from recognising Augustenburg. The Austrians had little option but to co-operate with Prussia. Their policy of Confederate reform had failed, Napoleon's plans for a revision of the Vienna settlement threatened their position in Europe and, fearing the consequences of a triumph of German nationalism in Schleswig-Holstein, they wished to maintain the Olmütz agreement. Austria was therefore on the defensive and was to be consistently outmanocuvred by Bismarck (**107, 124, 126**).

Throughout December Austria and Prussia tried with only limited success to moderate the Confederation's enthusiasm for Augustenburg. They had agreed to the temporary occupation of Holstein by Confederate forces, but when Augustenburg set up court unofficially at Kiel, in Holstein, the Dual powers had little option but to act independently if they were to forestall a Confederate invasion of Schleswig and a *de facto* recognition of Augustenburg. On 17 January 1864 the Austro-Prussian Convention was signed and their troops crossed the Eider into Schleswig.

Bismarck's immediate concern was to isolate the battlefield in Schleswig from possible great power intervention until Denmark had been decisively defeated. While he may have exaggerated the dangers of intervention, he nevertheless needed to proceed with great caution. Later he compared himself to a hunter in a marsh who 'never advanced a foot until certain that the ground . . . is firm and safe' (**30**, p. 239). In February, for example, he had to control the impetuosity of the aged and eccentric (**95**) commander of the Prussian forces, von Wrangel, until he had gained Austrian agreement to carry the war over the Danish frontier into Jutland. Then in March, when Britain proposed an international conference in London, Bismarck skilfully delayed its meeting until the Prussian army had decisively defeated the Danes at Düppel, so strengthening his position at the conference table.

Bismarck had consistently made Prussian recognition of the Treaty of London dependent on Denmark's strict fulfilment of its clauses. At the London Conference the aggressive miscalculations of the King of Denmark played straight into his hands. The Danes, believing that they enjoyed international support, stubbornly refused to restore the autonomy of Schleswig and consequently enabled the Dual Powers to repudiate the Treaty and gain freedom of action. The British Cabinet refused to endorse the bellicosity of its Prime Minister, Palmerston, and the Danes were left isolated when the armistice expired on 26 June 1864. They were defeated within days and surrendered the duchies to the Dual Powers.

Denmark's refusal to compromise had confronted Austria with a serious dilemma: ultimately Augustenburg's claims would have to be recognised or the duchies ceded to Prussia. Initially unable to countenance the inevitable strengthening of Prussia that annexation would entail, Austria chose the former course even before the London Conference had ended. To avoid a rupture with Austria, Bismarck had to agree, but he insisted on such substantial constitutional concessions from Augustenburg that inevitably they were declined as they were tantamount to a virtual Prussian annexation. The ultimate fate of the duchies was left undecided and they were ruled provisionally by a fragile Austro-Prussian condominium.

During the next two years Bismarck's diplomacy was at its most complex. His simultaneous pursuit of alternative and sometimes contradictory policies makes interpretation particularly difficult. Recent detailed research has to some extent 'unravelled the logic that lay behind [these] sudden changes of policy' (**36**) by showing how he would keep his alternatives open until it was clear which one offered the maximum advantage and the least risk. It has, however, been argued that too much stress on 'the strategy of alternatives' (**30**, p. 237) exaggerates the element of conscious planning in Bismarck's diplomacy. Crankshaw (**22**, pp. 176–7), for example, argues that Bismarck's thoughts were 'capable of existing in a state of something very like suspension . . . with all the ingredients hovering invisibly in solution until the right temperature is reached, the right catalyst introduced, to crystallise them beautifully out'. While Bismarck did not have an exact blueprint for action, he did have certain basic aims of which he never lost sight. He was working towards the annexation of Schleswig-Holstein and ultimately Prussian hegemony in North Germany.

Austria was now the main hindrance to a Prussian annexation of the duchies, but Bismarck was in no hurry to force the issue as time appeared to be on Prussia's side. Austria was practically bankrupt, was threatened with war in Venetia, and was isolated both in Europe and within the German Confederation. It therefore suited Bismarck to maintain the alliance in the hope that the logic of Austria's position would persuade the Emperor to concede Prussian demands peacefully. In August 1864 King William and Bismarck met the Austrian Emperor and Rechberg, his Foreign Minister, at Schönbrunn. At ministerial level a verbal agreement was quickly reached whereby Prussia would gain the duchies in exchange for a guarantee of Venetia and help in the reconquest of Lombardy. However, when Rechberg produced a more precise draft of the agreement, both monarchs rejected it. Franz Joseph refused to cede the duchies to Prussia, while William was reluctant to ignore the legality of Augustenburg's claims. Bismarck's intentions were ambiguous. It is just possible that he was 'running full tilt after the conservative alliance' (**32**, p. 75) but the majority of historians are more sceptical of his motives. It is more likely that he never intended to commit Prussia to any precise obligations and was in fact trying to ensure the advantages of continued Austrian co-operation by 'dangl[ing] once more, as so often in the past, the enticing possibility of such bargain' (**30**, p. 251).

Even if Bismarck had genuinely been pursuing a conservative alliance, economic rivalry was making this, if not impossible, then at least more difficult to achieve. In October 1864, when the southern German states at last accepted the French Free-Trade Treaty as a condition for renewing the *Zollverein*, serious opposition to its re-negotiation disappeared. Bismarck had been anxious to mitigate the effects of this on Austro-Prussian relations by promising joint Austro-*Zollverein* negotiations some time before 1872 on a customs treaty, but the Prussian Finance Ministry, with the backing of the Crown, managed to prevent even this gesture (**32, 71**).

Throughout the winter of 1864–65 the future of Schleswig-Holstein remained undecided and Austro-Prussian relations steadily deteriorated. Rechberg had resigned as a result of his failure to gain any concessions from Prussia over the *Zollverein* and was replaced by Mensdorff-Pouilly. He increasingly accepted the anti-Prussian line of his department. In the duchies the Prussian Commissioner, Zedlitz, behaved with arrogance (**30**), while Bismarck consistently blocked any solution to their sovereignty which was not compatible with Prussian ambitions. In November Mensdorff gave Bismarck a choice between either recognising an independent Schleswig-Holstein under Augustenburg, or buying Austrian consent to Prussian annexation with territorial concessions in Silesia and the Hohenzollern enclaves of Württemberg. An answer was delayed until February, when Prussian recognition of

Augustenburg was again coupled with unacceptable conditions. These would have entailed a *de facto* Prussian annexation.

By April war seemed likely. Austria supported a motion in the Federal Diet to hand over Holstein to Augustenburg and Prussia countered by announcing the transfer of her main naval base from Danzig to Kiel. Yet Bismarck was still reluctant to risk war [**doc. 14**]. At the Prussian Crown Council of 29 May 1865 he was virtually alone in advising concessions to Austria, which were rejected by William. Bismarck's 'moderation' has been partly explained by Stern and Röhl who have shown that the Prussian government, unwilling to appeal to the *Landtag*, needed time to raise money elsewhere and to convince bankers that a loan to Austria would be a poor investment (**93, 123**). Bleichröder was successfully entrusted with the task of selling the Prussian state's share in the Cologne-Minden railway, and by July Bismarck was secure in the knowledge that 'the financial means for complete mobilisation and for a one-year military campaign [were] available' (**93**, p. 63) [**doc. 15**]. Nevertheless Bismarck still hesitated to go to war and in August responded to Austrian peace-feelers. At Bad Gastein a compromise, essentially inspired by Bismarck, was agreed to. Lauenburg was purchased outright by Prussia and the administration of the duchies was divided: Schleswig was to be governed from Berlin and Holstein from Vienna. The Austrians, however, insisted that joint sovereignty over the two duchies should remain intact [**doc. 16**]. Bismarck's reluctance to be stampeded into war was motivated by a desire to buy time both for further diplomatic, financial and military preparations and for his already considerable achievements in foreign affairs and in the *Zollverein* re-negotiations to mollify political opposition at home (**25**). Arguably Bismarck hoped that the Treaty, which by its very nature was only provisional, would lead to further Austrian concessions.

Co-operation between Prussia and Austria was only possible on the basis of a complete Austrian acknowledgement of Prussian hegemony north of the Main, but Franz Joseph was unwilling to make that concession. Bismarck recognised the crude logic of the situation when he offered the Austrian ambassador in October 1865 either 'a genuine alliance or war to the knife' (**32**, p. 81). Gastein failed to improve Austro-Prussian relations and consequently Bismarck continued to work towards isolating Austria and preparing for war without irrevocably committing himself to it. Early in October he took advantage of a visit to Biarritz to allay Napoleon's fears of a Prusso-Austrian rapprochement. Throughout the winter of 1865–66 friction continued unabated in the duchies. In Schleswig the Prussians tried to stamp out popular support for Augustenburg, while the Austrians pursued the opposite course in Holstein. When the Austrians permitted a pro-Augustenburg rally in Altona in January 1866, Bismarck dispatched what amounted to an ultimatum. This in effect was rejected. It appeared that Bismarck had now reached 'the line of hard resistance' (**30**, p. 261). Not surprisingly, at the Prussian Crown Council of 28 February 1866 it was agreed that war with Austria was inevitable and Bismarck, conscious that the real issue at stake was the future control of Germany rather than Schleswig-Holstein, urged that Prussia should proclaim herself the leader of German nationalism (**101**).

Definite preparations for war were now made. On 8 April Bismarck concluded an offensive alliance with Italy for a period of three months. On the following day a serious attempt was made to woo nationalist opinion when the Prussian representative at Frankfurt proposed the calling of a German parliament based on universal franchise. Throughout April and May the armies of Austria, Prussia and Italy began to mobilise, but even at this stage Bismarck kept his options open. The most serious attempt at mediation was a proposal made by the Gablenz brothers, one of whom was Governor of Holstein, to divide Germany along the Main line into Austrian and Prussian spheres of influence. There is considerable disagreement as to why Bismarck appeared to accept the Gablenz Plan as a basis for a settlement. It has been seen as essentially a tactical manoeuvre to head off the threat of French intervention, but it has also been strongly argued that Bismarck wanted to avoid a German civil war and genuinely desired an organic solution to German unification. Bismarck was never adverse to a diplomatic settlement which conceded the substance of his demands. He detailed an official to draft a secret memorandum in an attempt to square the circle of Austro-Prussian dual control and a national German parliament (**101**). In practice this would have enabled Prussia to control North Germany and be a dominant influence in the new parliament. Not surprisingly Austria rejected the Gablenz initiative at the end of May 1866.

The maverick policies of Napoleon III were a constant threat to Bismarck. Not only was Napoleon anxious to detatch Venetia from Austria, but he also hoped to gain Luxemburg and the Bavarian Rhineland by playing off Prussia against Austria. Despite attempts by a later generation of patriotic German historians to argue to the contrary, Bismarck did contemplate offering France limited territorial concessions since French neutrality was of paramount importance. (**25**).

The fear of Prussian domination rallied the majority of the lesser states to Austria. Only the Thuringian states, Oldenburg, the two Mecklenburgs and the cities of Hamburg, Bremen and Lübeck supported Berlin (**38**). On 1 June 1866 Vienna unilaterally broke the Gastein Treaty and appealed to the Confederation to solve the future of the duchies. Prussia retaliated by occupying Holstein, which the Austrians had evacuated, and by proposing a revolutionary plan for a *Kleindeutsch* union. The Austrians then took the final steps to war. On 11 June they called upon the lesser states to mobilise and hastily secured French neutrality by promising to cede Venetia to Italy and to agree a French satellite state on the Rhine. Prussia replied by declaring the Confederation dissolved and on 15 June her troops began to advance.

Bismarck was ready to use any weapon to achieve victory. Without hesitation he revived the most radical cries of 1848 and even persuaded the King to promise a national parliament elected by universal franchise. He also attempted 'to uncoil the springs of nationalistic discontent' (**30**, p. 302) within the Austrian empire by encouraging separatist movements. However, when on 3 July the Austrian army was defeated at Königgratz (**96**), he was equally anxious to terminate hostilities before Austrian forces could regroup and other powers were tempted to intervene. Indeed on the day before Königgratz Vienna had already requested French mediation. Bismarck struggled to restrain both the generals and the King, who desired further military operations, and finally persuaded them to accept French proposals for a short truce. He then induced William, Napoleon and Franz Joseph to accept a realistic peace, whilst simultaneously preparing for the possibility that Napoleon might suddenly be tempted into armed intervention against Prussia. Von Goltz, the Prussian ambassador in Paris, cleverly won over Napoleon by appealing to his vanity as mediator and by stressing that Prussia intended to respect the independence of the south German states. He also hinted unofficially that Bismarck might be willing to make some minor territorial concessions (**25**). Bismarck had immense difficulty in persuading the King to agree to the terms [**doc. 17**], but on 26 July 1866 the Preliminary Peace of Nikolausburg was signed.

In early August, belatedly responding to von Goltz's veiled offers, the French suddenly claimed the whole of the left bank of the Rhine up to Mainz. The sheer scale of these demands destroyed French credibility as protector of South German independence. It enabled Bismarck to threaten to unite the whole of Germany against Napoleon. He was also able to negotiate, as part of the individual peace treaties with Hesse-Darmstadt, Baden, Württemberg and Bavaria, military alliances ensuring Prussian control of their armies and railways in wartime (**30**). Napoleon gave way and on 23 August the Peace was confirmed at Prague.

Although Austria lost no territory except Venetia, Franz Joseph conceded Prussia a free hand in Germany and the replacement of the German Confederation by two new potential federations, north and south of the Main, in neither of which was Austria to be represented. Bismarck had hoped to include provision for their eventual union, but the French vetoed it. On 20 September 1866 Prussia annexed Hanover, Hesse Kassel, Nassau and the City of Frankfurt, all of which had been allies of Austria. Due to French pressure Saxony escaped absorption, although she was compelled to join the North German Confederation. The southern states remained independent, but as well as having to accept the military alliance with Prussia, they were charged indemnities and had to agree to re-negotiate the *Zollverein* on Prussian terms.

Bismarck, then, had exploited the weaknesses of his opponents with immense skill, but he had also operated in what was an essentially favourable European diplomatic environment (**121**) [**doc. 18**].

Part Three: The North German Confederation

6 The Creation of the North German Confederation, 1866–67

The Austrian defeat and the subsequent creation of the North German Confederation mark a major turning point in modern German history. Not only was the constitutional, economic and legal infrastructure of the future German *Reich* laid in the years 1866–70 but in the process the party political mould of the early sixties was permanently shattered (**34**).

When the first session of the newly elected Prussian *Landtag* opened in August 1866, the constitutional conflict was still unresolved. In the teeth of Cabinet opposition Bismarck persuaded the King to agree to an indemnity bill by which the Government would seek the *Landtag*'s retrospective approval for the expenditure of the last four years. The Liberals were as surprised by his evident desire to compromise as the ultra-Conservatives were infuriated by his refusal to exploit Königgratz to establish a neo-absolutist regime. The moderates in both main Liberal parties argued for its acceptance, believing that by co-operating with Bismarck, they would be able to influence his policies. The Left stressed that the bill would merely legalise four years' unconstitutional rule and would set a dangerous precedent for the future (**61**). The bill was passed by an overwhelming majority of 230 to 75 on 3 September 1866. The agonising debates it caused amongst the ranks of both the Progressives and the Conservatives led to a secession of moderates which in the course of the winter of 1866–67 crystallised into the National Liberal Party and the Free Conservative Party (**30, 61**).

In retrospect the moderate Liberals have been criticised for agreeing to the indemnity bill (**24**), but at the time any other choice was virtually impossible. They were in agreement with Bismarck's economic and foreign policy, and the successful outcome of the Austrian war had made them all too aware of the impotence of the parliamentary opposition. Realistically they accepted the need for co-operating with Bismarck in shaping the North German Confederation, as the attitude of the south Germans – at least temporarily – rendered national unification impossible [**doc. 19**]. In other words, 'three quarters of a loaf appeared better than none' (**67**, p. 295). Bismarck also had compelling reasons for ending the constitutional conflict. His diplomatic training had equipped him to view politics in terms of a balance of forces. He appreciated that the Liberals were still a force and that he would need their support to neutralise the considerable pockets of hostility in the newly annexed territories and to counter the particularism of the remaining independent states when it came to drafting the constitution of the North German Confederation.

The outright annexation of Hanover, Nassau, Hesse Kassel, Schleswig-Holstein and Frankfurt contrasted starkly with Bismarck's willingness to compromise with the Prussian *Landtag*. It was an arbitrary act reminiscent of Napoleon I (**30**) and clear confirmation that Prussia 'had no intention of merging into Germany' (**40**, p. 182). The provinces were initially occupied and somewhat brutally absorbed into the Prussian administrative system. Frankfurt was forced to pay a punitive indemnity and the ruling houses of Hanover, Hesse Kassel and Nassau were deposed.

Annexation was supported by the local Liberals who appreciated the material advantages of union with Prussia and realised that only armed intervention could have overcome stubborn local patriotism. Nevertheless, the initial experience of occupation, particularly in Hanover, was oppressive (**76 Vol. 2, 89, 90**). The press was censored, disloyal civil servants were suspended, and former Hanoverian soldiers with Guelph sympathies were imprisoned.

Up to the summer of 1867 a policy of crude Prussianisation was carried out. However, when in August the Crown Prince sharply warned of the mounting hostility towards Berlin in Hanover, Bismarck intervened and conceded a tolerable degree of local autonomy, which was later extended to Hesse-Kassel and Nassau. Bismarck could not afford to ignore the fact that aggressive Prussianisation would only stiffen the opposition of the south German states to eventual German unification.

Bismarck lost little time in drafting the constitution of the North German Confederation. In early August 1867 the rulers of the remaining independent states north of the Main were invited to Berlin to attend a 'congress of roaches presided over by a benevolent pike' (**26**, p. 225). On 18 August in a series of bilateral treaties with Prussia they agreed that a draft federal constitution would be submitted to a constituent assembly elected by direct universal manhood suffrage and that the armed forces of the states would come under the supreme command of the King of Prussia in his rôle as President of the North German Confederation.

Although some argue that 'seldom in history has a constitution been so clearly the product of the thought and will of a single individual' (**30**, p. 337), the political situation in 1867 imposed considerable restraints on Bismarck. He wanted to ensure the hegemony of Prussia, but at the same time needed to create 'an acceptable Prussian image south of the Main' (**67**, p. 296). The first draft of the constitution was ready by December. To make possible the eventual accession of the southern states it was 'designed to exact the minimum surrender of state sovereignty compatible with creating a viable framework within which a national state could evolve' (**67**, p. 298). The confederation consequently became responsible for defence and foreign policy and could legislate on such matters as customs, commerce, banking and civil and commercial law.

In essence the constitution was to consist of the Presidency (*Praesidium*), the Federal Council (*Bundesrat*) and Chamber of Deputies (*Reichstag*). Responsibility for foreign affairs, for the declaration of war and for the dismissal of Confederate officials was invested in the King of Prussia, who was also Supreme Commander of the armed forces. The *Bundesrat* was composed of representatives nominated by the member states of the Confederation and was created specifically to demonstrate a continuity with the former German Confederation. Voting procedure remained unchanged, as the states' representatives voted *en bloc* according to the instructions of their governments. Bismarck avoided stressing the massive preponderance of Prussia's power in North Germany by allotting her a modest but adequate total of seventeen seats out of forty-three in the *Bundesrat* (**67**); that was the number reached by adding together the votes Prussia and the states which she had annexed had commanded in the Frankfurt *Diet*. The *Bundesrat* had both legislative and executive functions. It could be convened independently of the *Reichstag*, initiate legislation and veto bills from the lower house. While bills had to be approved both by the *Bundesrat* and *Reichstag*, constitutional amendments required a two-thirds majority in the *Bundesrat*, which was impossible to secure without Prussian consent. The executive functions of the *Bundesrat* were to be carried out through committees dealing with particular areas of responsibility, which Bismarck assumed, but did not specifically state, would gradually evolve into Confederate departments or ministries (**30, 148**). Faithful to the model of the former German Confederation, the draft also initially envisaged that the Chancellor, the only federal minister to be created by the constitution, would merely preside over the *Bundesrat*. He would be appointed by Berlin and receive instructions from Bismarck acting in his rôle of Prussian Foreign Minister. Originally the Chancellorship was to have gone to the former Prussian delegate at Frankfurt, but Bismarck filled the post himself when its potential importance became clear. By remaining Prussian minister-president he secured himself a pivotal position within the constitution.

The rôle envisaged for the *Reichstag* emphasised 'the fundamental dilemma of his constitutional thinking' (**30**, p. 341). He wanted to win popular support for an essentially conservative constitution and create a potential check on the independence of the Crown and bureaucracy, without creating parliamentary government. Consequently there was to be universal male franchise. The lack of payment for deputies, however, was an attempt to ensure that the working man could in practice only vote for his social superiors. There was no provision for the rights of interpellation and petition, and the articles on taxation 'made a mockery of parliamentary budget rights' (**30**, p. 340). There was no annual budget or provision for parliamentary control of military expenditure. The Confederation was permitted to levy indirect taxation, but this ensured that once initial parliamentary approval had been gained, taxation would become automatic and increase as the economy expanded. The Confederation's income was to be supplemented by annual grants from the states.

Neither the individual states nor the Constituent *Reichstag* were able to alter the fundamental characteristics of Bismarck's draft constitution, which he most skilfully defended by playing off his opponents against each other. When Bismarck convened a conference in December 1866 to discuss the constitution in detail, the majority of the states, intent on increasing their own power, rallied behind a proposal put forward by the representatives of Oldenburg to create a proper Confederate cabinet and an upper house of princes, designed both to weaken Prussian influence and be a check on the *Reichstag*. Bismarck countered with his familiar stick and carrot technique. He mollified the opposition by granting the individual states minor concessions, but he also threatened to harness the democratic forces of the *Reichstag* if he failed to secure consent for the constitution.

The Constituent *Reichstag* was elected on 12 February 1867. Out of a possible 297 seats the National Liberals won 79, the Free Conservatives 39 and the Progressives a mere 19, while the Conservatives gained 59. The remainder went to the small particularist and nationalist splinter parties – the Poles, Danes, Guelphs and Ultramontanes*. When discussions began on the draft constitution, Bismarck reverted to his familiar tactics of playing off the *Reichstag* against the state governments. He raised the spectre of Liberal opposition to browbeat the state governments into defending the constitution. He secured their agreement to a secret treaty to dissolve the *Reichstag* and arbitrarily impose a constitution should Liberal opposition threaten ratification. Nevertheless the Liberals did win considerable concessions which 'removed some of the basic deficiencies of the Bismarck draft and gave the *Reichstag* many of the essential attributes of a modern parliamentary body' (**30**, p. 358).

Amendments were passed which increased the scope of the Confederation's legislative power. Bismarck also conceded legal immunity to members of the *Reichstag* during parliamentary sessions, voting by secret ballot in general elections and the commitment to hold elections 60 days after the dissolution of the *Reichstag*. He refused, however, to permit the payment of deputies.

The National Liberals sought to make both the Chancellor and the heads of the administrative committees set up by the *Bundesrat* legally responsible to the *Reichstag*. This did not entail parliamentary government in the British sense but rather the guarantee that the Chancellor and his leading officials would be legally responsible for the decisions they took. Bismarck feared that this could undermine his own power by recreating in the Confederation the Prussian tradition of collegiate responsibility. He consequently insisted that only the Chancellor, together with the President, should sign all laws and ordinances.

Bismarck readily conceded parliamentary control over an annual budget, but this by no means gave the *Reichstag* a complete grip on the Confederation's finances. Most of the Confederation's expenditure was earmarked for the military or 'iron' budget, which Bismarck refused to surrender to annual parliamentary control. After a deadlock which in early April placed the whole constitutional settlement in doubt, Bismarck negotiated a compromise with the National Liberals that was facilitated by the war scare over Luxemburg, and that safeguarded military expenditure for the next five years.

The North German Confederation

On 16 April 1867 the *Reichstag* finally ratified the amended constitution by 230 to 53. The constitution has never ceased to be the subject of controversy. Opinions have varied as to whether it was 'the Königgratz of liberalism in Germany' (**26**, p. 234), or whether in fact it made Germany 'a constitutional country' with a parliament that 'possessed every essential function' (**32**, p. 98). It is true that the National Liberals had extracted from Bismarck greater concessions than he intended to make, but until 1919 the executive was never successfully subjected to parliamentary control. Bismarck dominated the North German Confederation and twisted the constitution to suit his own political situation, but the settlement of 1866–67 was also very much a product of contemporary conditions. In that sense it was a genuine compromise between the conservative agrarian forces on one side and the more dynamic liberal business classes on the other (**25**). Arguably it only began to come under pressure when the conditions under which it was drafted changed.

7 Bismarck, Napoleon and the Southern States

Although the Treaty of Prague confirmed Prussian hegemony north of the Main, and by dissolving the German Confederation finally destroyed the basis of Habsburg influence in Germany, no permanent solution to the German problem had yet been found and consequently the situation remained unstable and dangerous (**30, 121**). The southern states were weak and divided and their close economic and military ties with the North German Confederation seemed to indicate that their absorption was only a matter of time, but it was also clear that any breach of the Main line would be bitterly opposed by the French. Napoleon, whose position depended on the prestige of his régime, could not afford to tolerate any further Prussian aggrandisement unless accompanied by substantial concessions from Berlin. Bismarck, however, was coming under increasing pressure from the National Liberals and Free Conservatives to complete unification without sacrificing an inch of German territory [**doc. 21**]. He was fortunate that there was little danger of a hostile European alliance forming. The powers were distracted by the Eastern question, which had re-emerged with the Cretan revolt in the summer of 1866. They remained in a state of 'diplomatic disorientation' (**121**, p. 253) from each other until 1868.

Bismarck's own attitude towards south Germany was ambiguous. Although French pressure was the real reason why he had halted at the Main, he considered the Catholic south as an essentially alien society, which would not integrate easily with the Protestant north. On the other hand he was aware of the dangers of a power vacuum in the south and of the impatient desire of the nationalists to complete unification. Taylor has argued that 'Bismarck had no clear aim after the victories of 1866 . . . he asked only to be left alone' (**32**, p. 102). In fact Bismarck developed a whole range of policies for accomplishing the gradual integration of the south by enmeshing it in a series of military, economic and constitutional links, which without overtly disturbing the status quo would eventually set up an irresistible momentum towards national unity (**25, 30, 71**).

After failing to gain the Palatinate in August 1866, Napoleon redoubled his efforts to win territorial concessions elsewhere from Prussia. Increasingly he focused on Luxemburg, which he was willing to purchase from the King of Holland, but as it had formed part of the German Confederation since 1814 it was garrisoned by Prussian troops. Bismarck's reaction to the French initiative was complex and opportunist. It is almost impossible to know whether he genuinely wanted a settlement with Napoleon or whether he deliberately provoked a major crisis 'in order to bring the new *Reichstag* to heel and strengthen his hold over the southern states' (**22**, p. 245). Retrospectively the French were convinced that Bismarck had set a trap for them but there is some evidence to suggest that initially Bismarck was not opposed to their purchase of the duchy. He certainly gave Napoleon careful advice on how to proceed, and, when the news of Napoleon's negotiations with the Dutch became public in March 1867, the first reaction of the papers closest to the Government was to play down the importance of Prussia's involvement in Luxemburg (**102**). It has been argued (**32**) that Bismarck hoped to appease Napoleon, so that he could concentrate on consolidating the North German Confederation without fear of French intervention. However, a crisis with France would also stimulate German patriotism and deflect Liberal criticism of the new constitution. Bismarck himself was scarcely a free agent. Once the *Reichstag* met he could not be seen to be encouraging Napoleon to purchase land which could be regarded as German.

Napoleon's best hope of success lay in acting quickly, but he missed the chance of achieving a quick settlement in September 1866 before Bismarck fell ill. When Bismarck returned to Berlin in December, he increasingly had serious doubts about the purchase, but nevertheless kept his options open. By February he seemed to want to spin out the affair for a further six months before risking a rupture with France, so that he would have time to consolidate north Germany and tighten the links with the south (**30**).

Napoleon opened negotiations with the Dutch King on 16 March. He also began a crude pro-French propaganda campaign in the duchy at a time which 'could hardly have been more convenient for Bismarck' (**30**, p. 379), as the *Reichstag* was debating the contentious issues of ministerial responsibility and parliamentary control of the 'iron' budget. On 1 April Bismarck faced an interpellation in the *Reichstag*, which he had very probably inspired, deploring the rumoured French purchase of Luxemburg. The subsequent explosion of nationalist wrath left little room for diplomatic manoeuvre. Under pressure from Berlin the Dutch refused to sell the duchy. Nevertheless, Bismarck did not want war with France [**doc. 20**] and despite exploiting the crisis over the next three weeks for domestic purposes, he indicated to the British that he would be ready to accept the mediation of the great powers. At the subsequent London Conference, a compromise was arranged whereby the Prussian garrison was withdrawn and the duchy was neutralised under a great-power guarantee. Although Napoleon had gained a significant military concession, it was out-weighed by the scale of the diplomatic defeat he had again suffered. The crisis had emphasised the growing tension between Prussia and France and can be seen as 'the dress rehearsal for the crisis of 1870' (**121**, p. 263). In retrospect the crisis appears to be a triumph of timing, yet it is more likely that Bismarck pursued his familiar 'strategy of alternatives' until his hand was finally forced in April 1867.

The Luxemburg crisis provided Bismarck with an opportunity to attempt to tighten the links between north and south Germany. He tried unsuccessfully to draw Bavaria into a special or 'constitutional' alliance with the north and also failed to breach the Main Line, being unable to persuade southern Hesse to join the North German Confederation. In the short term it was only economic pressure that secured Berlin an important but far from final victory over southern particularism. In the autumn of 1866 the south had agreed to negotiate a new customs union with the North German Confederation. As an interim measure the existing *Zollverein* remained in force but could be dissolved by Prussia at six months' notice. In June 1867 the ministers of the southern states were summoned to Berlin where, under threat of a dissolution of the *Zollverein*, they agreed to a radical revision of its constitution. Despite Bavarian opposition it was accepted that the existing General Congress and *liberum veto** should be replaced by a new council under the presidency of Prussia, and a democratically elected customs Parliament, in which members of the North German *Reichstag* and elected south German representatives would sit together (**71, 77**).

Bismarck had, perhaps rather naïvely, assumed that the self-evident material advantages of the *Zollverein* would quickly overcome southern particularism and lead the way to political union (**34, 71**). Bismarck had expected that the German nationalist parties would win big majorities when the elections for the *Zollverein* parliament were held in the southern states in February. However, he overestimated the influence of the businessmen, chambers of commerce and trade associations in the less industrialised south, and the elections resulted in a decided rebuff for Prussia. Forty-nine out of a possible eighty-five southern deputies were hostile to any attempt to widen the economic union into a political one. In Bavaria a strongly Catholic and particularist patriot party had emerged, whilst in Württemberg the People's Party, warning that any political union with Prussia would entail excessive taxation, conscription and 'keep[ing] your mouth shut' (**34**, p. 19), won every seat.

When the deputies assembled in Berlin in April 1868 it was therefore clear that there would be no quick evolution from an economic into a political union. Nevertheless it can be argued that the *Zollverein* parliament was of some psychological value to the cause of German unity as it brought southern and northern deputies who were elected by universal suffrage into direct contact with each other. Even particularists were now forced to stress their German rather than regional loyalties, although they still clung fiercely to the *status quo* and opposed any move towards unity (**30**).

During the next two years Bismarck appeared to accept that no immediate progress in German unity could be reached [**doc. 21**], but in practice he continued to exploit any chance as it arose and thus subtly and persistently undermined the Prague settlement. In the spring of 1868, for example, he welcomed a proposal by Hohenlohe, the Bavarian Minister-President, for creating a southern federation because he perceived that it would weaken the strong particularist traditions of the individual states. His train of thought was clearly revealed when he observed that 'the most difficult part of the task of national reconstruction is the removal of the existing. If what exists is breached, even though it be through a south German confederation, a healthy national life will grow by itself out of the ruins' (**30**, p. 405). It is not surprising therefore that both Württemberg and Bavaria eventually rejected the scheme.

Bismarck was more successful with plans for military integration. In February 1867 the southern states reluctantly agreed to Prussianise their armed forces and a year later decided on a joint mobilisation scheme. In 1869 Prussia, on the insistence of the pro-Prussian state of Baden, gained representation on the south German military committee administering the former confederate fortresses, which Bismarck optimistically believed would evolve into a German war cabinet.

By early 1870 the evolutionary approach to German unity seemed to have failed. Southern particularism showed no signs of weakening [**doc. 21**]. The Patriot Party had won a decisive victory in the Bavarian elections in November 1869, while a wave of anti-Prussian feeling swept Württemberg, culminating in a popular petition demanding the repeal of the Conscription Act of 1868. Simultaneously Bismarck was coming under pressure from the National Liberals in the *Reichstag* to complete unification. He was also increasingly aware that he would require parliamentary approval for renewing the 'iron' budget at the end of 1871 and that the more convincingly he could pose as the successful champion of German unity, the easier its passage would be. He therefore attempted in vain to persuade the southern states to approve King William's adoption of the title Emperor of Germany. He needed 'to give Germany a new "dose" of national enthusiasm' (**32**, p. 115). A major diplomatic success would probably have sufficed but victorious war was by no means excluded (**93**).

8 The Franco-Prussian War and the Unification of Germany, 1870–71

The extent and motivation of Bismarck's involvement in the candidacy of Prince Leopold of Hohenzollern-Sigmaringen for the Spanish throne, which was the immediate cause of the Franco-Prussian war, remains a controversial question. Despite some leaks in the 1890s (**117**), only in 1945 did it become possible to analyse Bismarck's involvement in detail when the relevant files, which had hitherto been denied to historians by the German Government, fell into the hands of the Allies and were published in 1957 (**7**). However, even this material, whilst confirming beyond doubt Bismarck's complicity, failed to show conclusively that he was aiming at war – his 'favourite garment was never the straight-jacket but the reversible overcoat' (**30**, p. 437). Kolb (**113**) has argued that Bismarck underestimated the hostile reaction the candidature would unleash in France. Other historians stress that Bismarck exploited it either to weaken Napoleon by precipitating an internal political crisis (**106**), or to isolate the hawks within the French Cabinet, thereby strengthening the Liberals who were inclined to tolerate the unification of Germany (**34, 110**). A consensus of recent research indicates that Bismarck knowingly risked war, even though he probably hoped to avoid it, as there appeared no other way of accelerating the unification of Germany (**111**) [**doc. 21**].

Bismarck's opportunity to intervene in Spanish politics occurred following the *coup* in Madrid in September 1868. Queen Isabella abdicated and the Provisional Government decided to replace the Bourbons with a new ruling dynasty, a decision welcomed by Bismarck as it removed a traditionally Francophile dynasty from power. After unsuccessful attempts to find Portuguese and Italian candidates, General Prim, the Spanish Minister-President, sounded out Prince Leopold, a member of the south German and Catholic branch of the Prussian royal family, to whom in February 1870 a formal offer was made. Leopold finally accepted in early June, after considerable pressure from Bismarck, who refused to be deterred by King William's scepticism and who subtly played upon the Hohenzollern-Sigmaringen sense of duty and ambition.

Bismarck had by now 'deliberately set sail on a collision course with the intent of provoking either war or a French internal collapse' (**30**). He had already received several veiled warnings from the French ambassador, and an informed article in an influential Viennese newspaper in April reported that Napoleon had warned the Spanish ambassador in Paris that Leopold's accession would lead to war. Bismarck was also aware of the hawkish and mercurial nature of Gramont, the new French foreign minister. It is therefore significant that on 6 June 1870 Bismarck informed Major Max von Versen, his agent in Madrid, that 'complications' with France were exactly what he was 'looking for' (**111**, p. 85).

Bismarck had hoped that Leopold's candidature would be quickly ratified by the *Cortes**, thereby presenting the French with a *fait accompli* (**30**). A muddle over dates by a cypher clerk in the Prussian embassy, however, led to an unexpected delay, during which the secret reached Paris. King William, alarmed at the bellicose reaction in Paris, persuaded Leopold to stand down. Bismarck was only saved from the greatest reverse in his career by Gramont's failure to perceive the extent of his own success. Gramont rashly insisted on the provision of guarantees against a renewal of the candidacy, but when William was confronted by the French ambassador at Ems on 13 July he refused and promptly sent an account of the interview to his Chancellor [**doc. 22a**]. Bismarck was probably more intent on warding off defeat than on precipitating war, and published in the German and European press an edited version of the Ems telegram which emphasised the rebuff delivered to the ambassador [**doc. 22b**]. Eyck has argued that its publication was tantamount to a declaration of war (**24**). On 13 July the French Cabinet had in fact already agreed to compromise on the guarantees, but the Ems telegram so infuriated the war party at Court, the nationalist deputies and public opinion that a diplomatic settlement was impossible and Napoleon was driven to declare war on 15 July. On the other hand the telegram was a 'clear statement of the facts' (**32**, p. 121). Bismarck did not invent William's refusal and it can be said with some justice that responsibility for the war 'rests not on one side or the other but squarely on both' (**111**, p. 91).

Once war was declared Bismarck had three priorities. He had to ensure that it could be fought and won in isolation, whilst simultaneously exploiting the outburst of patriotism to complete German unity. Then he had to devise a peace treaty which would quickly terminate hostilities whilst providing Germany with a secure western frontier.

As in 1864 and 1866, the international situation continued to favour Prussia (**121, 126**). Neither Austria nor France was able to create a viable anti-Prussian bloc. Beust, the Austrian foreign minister, failed to engineer an Austro-Russian conflict in the Near East, which he had hoped would involve Prussia, as Russia's only ally, and lead to the recreation of the Crimean alliance in the West. Napoleon was unable to create a triple alliance with Italy and Austria despite the conclusion of a draft agreement in May 1869. In reality the Italians would not co-operate until France had withdrawn her garrison from Rome, which guaranteed the independence of the Papacy – a step Napoleon could not easily contemplate as he needed Catholic support at home. The Austrians would not commit themselves without Italy, since they needed to secure their southern frontier before risking war with Prussia (**127**). In July 1870, therefore, both Austria and Italy remained neutral; Franz-Joseph kept his options open by partially mobilising, but the Italian Cabinet maintained its neutrality, even when Napoleon belatedly evacuated Rome in August. Bismarck had little to fear in the short term from either Russia or Britain. The Tsar reaffirmed his 1869 commitment to occupy Galicia in the event of Austrian intervention, and Britain, suspicious of Napoleon's ambitions in Belgium, was reassured by Prussian promises to respect Belgian neutrality (**121**).

Had the Prussians suffered any serious military reverse the dangers of the war escalating into a European conflict involving the great powers would have increased. However, luck, the skill of the Prussian General Staff (**97**), the effectiveness of the new Krupp field batteries and the superior morale of the Prussian troops ensured a rapid series of French defeats culminating in the great Prussian victory of Sedan in September, which at least temporarily discouraged the threat of foreign intervention (**97**). Despite the collapse of the Bonapartist regime Bismarck attempted initially to negotiate both with Napoleon, who was captured at Sedan, and with the Empress, who had fled to England. He hoped to persuade Napoleon to cede Alsace and northern Lorraine in return for the freedom to employ the remaining Imperial army, which was besieged at Metz, to restore him to the throne. The Prussian generals were suspicious of Bismarck's peace initiative, as they desired first to complete the annihilation of the French armies. They consequently refused to co-operate in the delicate process of unofficial discussions with either Napoleon or the new Government of National Defence (**95, 99**) [**doc. 24**].

It was not, however, primarily the army which prevented an early peace but rather the demand for Alsace-Lorraine, the annexation of which was to fuel French desire for *revanche* over the next half-century. Opinions are divided on whether Bismarck was forced by popular nationalism and military pressure into annexation (**108**) or whether he himself manipulated the press and public opinion into voicing this demand (**22, 116**). Craig has attempted to synthesise the debate by observing 'an objective view of the evidence would seem to indicate that neither public opinion nor Bismarck needed inducement' (**34**, p. 29). There is little doubt that annexation was popular. At the start of the war nationalist journals in both north and south Germany began to call for the liberation of these two predominantly German-speaking provinces which had been annexed by Louis XIV and XV. Although not completely immune to nationalist argument, Bismarck nevertheless regarded Alsace and northern Lorraine as a vital strategic barrier against future French attacks (**99, 108**). He showed surprisingly little interest in the Lorraine iron ore deposits (**88**).

The war, with all its attendant uncertainties and dangers, dragged on until the fall of Paris in January 1871. While two Prussian armies were tied up around Paris, their communications were harassed by partisans [**doc. 23**], and ominously the Government of National Defence began to prepare for a people's war. By December 'the prestige of Sedan was dribbling away and with it all hope of securing a peace as cheap and successful as that which followed Sadowa' (**97** p. 388). It was becoming increasingly difficult to ensure the continued diplomatic isolation of the conflict. In late October, when Russia, in defiance of Britain and Austria, unilaterally repudiated the clauses in the 1856 Treaty enforcing the neutralisation of the Black Sea, a major European crisis erupted which threatened a Near Eastern war that would almost certainly have coalesced with the Franco-Prussian conflict. Bismarck skilfully defused the crisis by proposing an international conference in London where a face-saving formula for Britain and Austria could be devised. He thwarted French attempts to have the Franco-Prussian war discussed by securing prior agreement from the other powers to leave it off the agenda of the conference in return for his services as an 'honest broker' (**121, 126**).

It has been argued that the final unification of Germany was a consequence of these growing diplomatic and military uncertainties rather than the main object of the war (**32**). The creation of the German Empire did, of course, ensure the continued participation of the southern states in the war, but the evidence suggests that Bismarck exploited the war as 'a sudden blessed opportunity to complete the work of national unification which he had feared would remain unfinished for years' (**76 Vol. 2** p. 417). Although the war was initially accompanied by an upsurge of nationalist feeling throughout the south, unification was not the result of sustained popular pressure but ultimately the recognition by the two major southern states, Bavaria and Württemberg, that in an era of Franco-German hostility 'the price of independence was political isolation, economic decline and military insecurity' (**76 Vol. 2** p. 421). After Sedan, Bavaria agreed to join the North German Confederation, but only in return for concessions which would seriously have weakened its cohesion. Although Bismarck recognised that the south had to be persuaded rather than conquered (**67**), he did not hesitate behind the scenes to threaten Bavaria with economic and political isolation (**30**). By hinting at a unilateral termination of the *Zollverein* treaty, and by inviting the other southern states to Versailles in October to discuss unity, he forced the Bavarian Cabinet to adopt a more flexible attitude. Bismarck exploited the differences between the individual states and negotiated separately with them. In practice he made considerable concessions, which strengthened the federal element in the constitution of 1867, although they fell far short of Bavaria's original demands.

The power of the individual states benefited from the increased authority of the *Bundesrat*. Now the *Bundesrat* had to give its approval before war could be declared or action taken against a rebellious member state. A new ruling meant that a vote of fourteen rather than, as originally, two-thirds could block any constitutional amendment, putting a veto within reach of the southern states if they could form a common front. Special concessions to Baden, Bavaria and Württemberg also authorised local taxation and administration of the postal and telegraph systems, while the two latter states were allowed to maintain their own armies in peacetime.

Although these concessions 'helped preserve a climate in which particularism would remain respectable' (**67** p. 300), the *Bundesrat* nevertheless remained a 'camouflage for Prussian supremacy' (**42** p. 159). As Prussia commanded seventeen out of a total fifty-eight votes, she could effectively veto any constitutional change. Prussian and *Reich* institutions were closely enmeshed at executive level: the Emperor was the King of Prussia, the Chancellor was the Prime Minister, foreign minister and head of the Prussian delegation to the *Bundesrat*, whilst the Prussian army, despite the 'decorative' (**30**, p. 488) concessions to Bavaria and Württemberg, was in reality the German army. At the end of November the southern states had agreed to union, and King Louis of Bavaria was bribed to invite William to accept the title of Emperor. By January 1871 the necessary legislation had passed both the Southern Parliaments and the North German *Reichstag* where, despite initial demands by the Progressives for a more liberal constitution and reservations by the National Liberals on the concessions to southern particularism, the government gained a large majority. William's reluctance to make such a radical break with tradition was finally overcome, and on 18 January 1871 the Empire was proclaimed in the Hall of Mirrors at Versailles.

During these complex constitutional negotiations tension continued to grow between Bismarck and the generals [**doc. 24**]. Bismarck was determined to start peace talks once Paris had fallen, whereas the 'politically illiterate' [**22**, p. 290] von Moltke resented diplomatic considerations which hampered plans for the further vigorous prosecution of the war. In mid-January, when the fall of Paris was imminent, Moltke drew up a draft surrender document which was so draconian that it would have strengthened the French will to resist. Bismarck, appalled at Moltke's lack of diplomacy, successfully persuaded William to grant him full responsibility for the armistice negotiations (**95, 99**). Bismarck, who had consistently kept in contact with Napoleon and the Empress, was then able to exert pressure on the Government of National Defence at Bordeaux to agree to an immediate armistice in return for recognition as the lawful government of France. On 25 January 1871 a three-week armistice was signed to enable elections to be held for a National Assembly. When it met it voted overwhelmingly for peace.

When the Preliminary Peace was signed on 26 February 1871 the Germans extracted stiff terms. Alsace and northern Lorraine – including the key fortress of Metz, which was added for strategic reasons – were annexed. An indemnity of five milliard francs was also to be paid over four years, after which the army of occupation in the eastern provinces would be withdrawn. The peace was confirmed by the Treaty of Frankfurt in May. Unlike the Prague Treaty of 1866 it was no triumph for moderation.

Bismarck had insisted on arbitrary annexation unlegitimised by referenda, which 'cemented the enmity it was supposed to be the consequence of' (**92** p. 146). Bismarck feared future French aggression and observed that 'an enemy whose honest friendship can never be won, must at least be rendered somewhat less harmful' (**30**, p. 479). In retrospect few would disagree that this was 'a miscalculation of great consequence' (**108**, p. 367) [**doc. 25**].

Part Four: The Second *Reich*: The Economic and Constitutional Context

9 The *Reich* and Prussia

Up to his resignation in 1890 Bismarck dominated *Reich* government. Under the direction of Rudolph Delbrück, the *Reich* Chancellor's office carried out the routine administration of the *Reich* and provided a nucleus for the growth of a national bureaucracy (**54 Vol. 4**). By 1880 it was divided into five separate departments, each under a secretary of state. Bismarck jealously maintained a tight grip on the office, which constitutionally was an extension of his Chancellorship. He 'abhorred the idea of collective government' (**148**, p. 22) and only twice did he call a meeting of state secretaries to discuss policy.

Theoretically Bismarck's position was less secure in the Prussian Cabinet. As the King, in Bismarck's own words, was still regarded as 'the real *de facto* Minister-President' (**148**, p. 22), majority decisions were not binding on the Cabinet and Bismarck's colleagues could at any time appeal to the King against him. In 1872 Bismarck experimented by surrendering the post of Minister-President, but found that this led to such, friction between the *Reich* and Prussia that within five months he resumed it (**34**). In practice Bismarck's virtually unshakeable influence on William ensured his own authority as long as the old King lived [**doc. 26**].

It was essential that Bismarck should control both the *Reich* and Prussian governments, because to the south Germans Bismarck's unique position was the only guarantee they possessed that the '*Reich* institutions were [not] simply a front for Prussian domination' (**148**, p. 25). As the rôle of the *Reich* Chancellor's office expanded, friction between the *Reich* and the individual states grew. Prussian ministers particularly resented not being consulted by Delbrück on the drafting of new *Reich* laws, when their co-operation would later be crucial to the laws' execution. So in 1878 Bismarck attempted radically to improve *Reich*-Prussian relations by proposing in the Deputy bill the abolition of the *Reich* Chancellery and its replacement with new departments which would be jointly run by both the *Reich* and Prussia. He intended to extend the existing union between the Prussian King and German Emperor and Prussian Minister-President and Chancellor to the whole Imperial bureaucracy. Arguably 'tension between the national government and that of Germany's most important state would be lessened and might eventually be eliminated' (**67**, p. 307). It is not surprising, however, that there was vigorous opposition from the non-Prussian-state delegations in the *Bundesrat* and the federalist parties in the *Reichstag* which effectively defeated the measure. Bismarck therefore had to ensure Prussian co-operation by the cruder method of dismissing recalcitrant ministers and replacing them with his own nominees.

Bismarck failed to find a long-term solution for effectively controlling the centrifugal tendencies within the *Reich*. By force of personality and influence he was able to hold the federal structure together, but the danger remained 'that under a different monarch and a different Chancellor the old disunity would reassert itself' (**148,** p. 23) and that a future German government would be confronted by the conflicting pressures of a Conservative Prussia where the continued existence of the three-class voting system ensured after 1878 a large Conservative majority in the *Landtag*, and a more left-wing *Reichstag* voted in on universal franchise.

10 The Financial Crash of 1873 and the Great Depression

Modern economic historians have warned against interpreting the Great Depression of 1873–96 'as the grand climacteric of the century, leading to a protectionist, illiberal, highly cartelized ... and externally aggressive economy and society' (**82**, p. 22). Nevertheless it marks an important turning point in the history of the Second Empire, where it was a catalyst for far-reaching political, economic and social changes (**84, 85**).

The successful compromise of 1866–67 between Liberalism and the Prussian Crown had been greatly facilitated by the unprecedented prosperity of the sixties (**76(2)**). After 1871 the boom initially seemed set to continue (**34, 49, 140**). The *Gründerjahre** of 1871–73 witnessed an annual productivity increase of nearly 5 per cent. As a result of the growth in railway construction, as many iron and steel works were built between 1870 and 1875 as had been over the preceding seventy years. Expansion was helped both by the generous credit policies of the banks and by the liquid capital injected into the economy by the punctual payment of the French indemnity. This was used to finance public works and military projects and to pay off war loans.

The availability of easy credit and the currency reform of 1871, which added some 762,000,000 marks to the amount of free capital in the economy, fuelled a major speculative boom. A large number of unsound limited companies were set up. By exaggerating their commercial prospects in the general financial euphoria of the times they had little difficulty in selling their shares at inflated rates [**doc. 27**]. As in 1929, there followed a spectacular crash. Confidence was first shaken by revelations in the *Reichstag* of the fraudulent practices of the successful Jewish speculator, Dr Strousberg (**83**), but it was the collapse of the Viennese stock market in April 1873 and the financial crisis in America that finally touched off a whole string of bankruptcies in Germany in the autumn (**70**). The collapse of the European capital market led to a slowing up of economic growth and a decline in business confidence that did not recover until the mid-nineties. Although the severity of the slump has been exaggerated, it was the first serious check to growth since 1852. Only in 1880 did production achieve the levels of 1872–73 and it began to falter again between 1882–86 and 1890–95 (**84, 140**).

Despite the depression the foundations of Germany's later technological supremacy were nevertheless laid in the eighties (**42, 72, 80**). In contrast to the rest of Europe large sums were invested in such pioneering inventions as the Gilchrist-Thomas steelmaking process, which enabled German industrialists to exploit local low-grade iron-ore to undercut foreign competition. Due to increased mechanisation and rationalisation, there were large increases in productivity during this decade in the textile, coal, iron and steel industries. As the average growth rate of the economy in the eighties was 2.5 per cent per annum it can be argued that 'there is no way in which the term "Great Depression" can have any meaning when applied to Germany after 1880' (**82**, pp 22–3). Neither did the depression halt the continuing migration of the population in the rural east Elbian provinces to Berlin and the Ruhr. This was being accelerated by the introduction on the *Junkers*' estates of modern machinery, and the planting of potatoes and sugar beet which were more effectively harvested by cheap immigrant Polish labour employed on a seasonal basis (**47**) [**docs. 28, 29**]. The eighties was the decade in which industry for the first time began to employ more workers than agriculture. Between 1880 and 1890 the number of cities with a population of over one hundred thousand increased from fifteen to twenty-six and by 1910 Germany had nearly as many large cities as the whole of the rest of the Continent [**doc. 28(c)**].

The depression also brought about structural changes in German industry (**72**). In order to streamline production and counter the effect of sinking prices, large engineering and steel firms like Borsig and Krupp began to expand vertically by acquiring coal and iron-ore mines, while many other industries such as cement, textiles and chemicals formed *kartells** which helped to stabilise prices and production. Between 1875 and 1890 over two hundred *kartells* were set up, setting a trend that was to continue into the Third *Reich*. The increasing concentration of German industry into large units produced an elite of powerful industrialists and bankers who were to form a close alliance with the aristocratic Prussian ruling class (**140**).

Inevitably the economic crisis shifted 'the centre of gravity of political agitation . . . from issues of political policies, from national unification and constitutional reconstruction . . . . . . to a crude emphasis on economic objectives' (**84**, p. 64). Pressure from the industrialists and the east Elbian Junkers, who were both anxious to preserve their share of the home market, was an important factor in Bismarck's decision to abandon free trade in 1879 (**80**). The successful campaign against free trade was initiated in 1871 by the League for the Protection of the Economic Interests of Rhineland and Westphalia – the so-called Long-name Society – and the Southern Union of German Textile Industrialists (**34**). They were powerfully reinforced in November 1873 by the League of German Iron and Steel Industrialists, which quickly built up a national network of committees representing some 214 firms. In 1876 a still more formidable pressure group emerged when leading industrialists founded the Central Association of German Industrialists. By appealing to both commercial and nationalist sentiments with the argument that Germany should be as self-sufficient as possible, the protectionists gradually won over the local chambers of commerce. In September 1875 they even convinced the Congress of German Economists, which had hitherto been a 'citadel of free-traders' (**71**, p. 371).

The protectionists were unable to exert effective pressure on the government until they had won the support of the powerful east Elbian farming lobby. Initially the *Junkers* had welcomed the fall in the price of industrial goods, but by 1875 German farmers were experiencing keen competition from imported American and Russian grain and even wool from Australia. This had been made possible by the construction of railways in the Prairies and southern Russia and vastly improved shipping services (**80**). In 1876 Germany became a net importer of grain and east Elbian agriculture faced bankruptcy [**doc. 30**]. The political consequences of the agrarian crisis were highly explosive, as the traditional Prussian ruling elite was directly threatened. The first step in the campaign to protect agriculture was taken when a group of predominantly east Elbian landowners set up the League for Tax and Economic Reform in 1876. Initial co-operation with the industrial pressure groups was impeded by the League's conviction that only those with broad acres could effectively regenerate Germany and its essentially anti-business ethos, which desired the repeal of most of Bismarck's commercial legislation since 1862 (**71**) [**doc. 31**]. Nevertheless ever-increasing foreign competition rapidly brought about an effective working partnership between the agrarians and the industrialists. In February 1877 industrialists and farmers in Westphalia drew up a general declaration in favour of protective tariffs [**doc. 32**], and in October the Central Association and the League agreed on a detailed tariff scale for industrial and agricultural imports which not only ensured a successful assault on free trade (**80**), but also laid the foundations of the alliance between the Junkers and heavy industrialists which was to dominate late Wilhelmine politics.

The depression also played a part in bringing together the forces of the Left. Although as early as 1867 the Elberfeld and Barmen Chamber of Commerce reported that 'the working class is awaking from its dull apathy' (**76 Vol. 2**, p. 359), initially the patriotic fervour aroused by Sedan and the benign effects of full employment militated against left-wing politics. In the years immediately after 1873, however, the fear of redundancies, wage cuts and a constant feeling of insecurity created ever-growing support for a mass working-class movement. The two leading working-class parties, the General German Workers Union and the League of Workers' Clubs, co-operated in the election of 1874 and a year later united to form the Social Democratic Party (*SPD**). In the 1877 election the party polled nearly 10 per cent of the popular vote, and won twelve seats in the *Reichstag* (**56, 85**) [**doc. 34**].

The German industrial revolution did not impose the crude suffering of its British prototype. Although the new towns were brash and ugly and the workers lived in expensive and crowded tenements (**56**) [**doc. 33**], the availability of work (at least in the eighties), static or even sinking food prices [**doc. 35**] and the growing awareness of both the government and big business that socialism could only be contained by a state welfare policy, created conditions far removed from early nineteenth-century Manchester. Arguably the real cost of the industrial revolution was the cultural and psychological trauma it inflicted on the Germans, which showed itself in 'the violent resentments against the new industrialism, which in different guises erupted time and time again' (**91**, Introd.). The crash of 1873 provided 'a golden opportunity for prophets of disaster' (**84**, p. 60) as it discredited both economic and political liberalism and enabled the Conservatives and survivors of the pre-capitalist era successfully to attack the Liberal ethos. Owing to their prominence in banking and on the stock exchange the Jews became the scapegoats for the crash and the symbol of all that was destroying the familiar pattern of the pre-industrial lifestyle (**85**). Anti-semitism developed into an economic and political mass movement, and in 1890 five deputies campaigning on a specifically anti-semitic programme were elected to the *Reichstag* [**doc. 34**]. Measured in economic terms the depression may indeed have been mild, but it irreparably damaged liberalism and rallied behind the Conservatives strong anti-modernist forces, which equated liberalism and democracy with a Jewish conspiracy.

Part Five: Domestic Politics

11 The *Kulturkampf* and the Decline of the National Liberals

In 1871 the National Liberals, and to a lesser extent the Progressives, were still the natural parliamentary allies of Bismarck and co-operated closely in creating the administrative and legal infrastructure of the new *Reich* by supporting bills for a national coinage, a new commercial code, the creation of a central bank and the introduction of a uniform legal procedure. The Conservatives were uncertain and divided in their reaction to the creation of a modern secular state (**52**) and suspicious that Bismarck had become 'the stirrup holder of Liberalism' (**25**, p. 468). The *Zentrum**, which was founded in December 1870, attracted the south German Catholics, the Poles and the other nationalist minorities, and was inevitably particularist in sympathy and a strong defender of federalism.

Taylor has argued that it was difficult to say between 1871 and 1877 whether 'Bismarck or the National Liberals determined the character of German policy' (**32**, p. 160). It is undeniable that 'the Government was drawn in a liberal direction in the early seventies' (**58**, p. 73), but the limits of the Liberals' influence were revealed whenever Bismarck's intentions diverged from their own. Bismarck, for example, pointedly refused to force a constitution on the reactionary state of Mecklenburg. Even the Prussian local government reforms of 1872 and 1875, which were bitterly opposed by the Prussian aristocracy, in fact reflected Bismarck's genius for granting concessions 'in form but not in substance' (**52**, p. 10), as the *Junkers* were still able to retain much of their power in the county and provincial diets. The Liberals' ideological struggle with the *Zentrum* and their desire to support a national policy weakened their will to oppose the government even on the most fundamental issues. Refusing to contemplate a temporary alliance with the *Zentrum*, which was worse than 'the kiss of death' (**50**, p. 190), they failed in 1874 to defeat an authoritarian press law, which empowered the government to imprison newspaper editors for publishing sensitive information, and they weakly agreed to a septennial rather than annual military budget (**34**).

The fanaticism with which the Liberals persecuted the Catholics is only explicable if viewed within the context of the struggle between the Liberal and Catholic movements to shape the cultural and social framework of German society (**54 Vol. 4**). In the sixties the south German Liberals were strongly anti-clerical. In Baden, for example, the Church Law of 1860 and the Elementary School Law of 1868 curtailed the freedom of the Roman Catholic Church within the state (**74**). The tradition of German Liberalism was anti-Catholic. Many of the leading Liberals were the sons of Protestant pastors and 'the historiography they learned at their mothers' knees depicted Luther as a national and liberal as well as a religious hero' (**50**, p. 197). Their inherent distrust of Catholicism was fuelled by the uncompromising nature of the contemporary papacy. In 1864 the *Syllabus Errorum* sweepingly condemned the doctrines which Liberals all over Europe believed formed the essential basis of a free society, and in 1870 the Vatican Council further offended Protestant opinion by promulgating the dogma of Papal Infallibility, which was even opposed by the majority of Catholic bishops in Germany (**75**).

It is puzzling that Bismarck should have launched so divisive a campaign as the *Kulturkampf** instead of attempting to integrate the large Catholic minority peacefully into the new *Reich*. His attitude towards the Catholics was essentially pragmatic. In 1870, when Italian troops occupied Rome, he even considered the diplomatic advantages of offering the Pope asylum in Germany. The *Zentrum* 'could have been an excellent engine for integrating discontented foreign and German particularists into the new Empire' (**50**, p. 145).

The 'new orthodoxy' (**73**, p. 16) in German historiography sees the *Kulturkampf* as a classic example of Bismarck's technique of 'negative integration' whereby he attempted to unite the Protestant majority in the *Reichstag* against 'the Roman menace' and deflect the Liberals from pursuing awkward constitutional questions (**49, 64, 86**). There is little doubt that Bismarck did exploit the political advantages afforded by the *Kulturkampf*, but this interpretation underestimates his genuine fear that the *Zentrum*, which was led by Windthorst, already an effective spokesman of popular particularism, was the natural rallying point for the enemies of *Kleindeutschland* – the Poles, the Bavarian Patriots and the inhabitants of Alsace-Lorraine [**doc. 36**].

Since the key areas of education and religion were state rather than *Reich* responsibilities (**74**), the *Kulturkampf* was waged principally by the Prussian government, with parallel struggles in Baden and Hesse. In 1871 the Catholic division of the Prussian Ministry of Culture was abolished and in January its Conservative minister was replaced by Adalbert Falk (**50**). The most important element of Prussia's *Kulturkampf* legislation was contained in the May Laws of 1873, which extended state control over the education of the clergy, undermined the authority of the Papacy by setting up a Royal Tribunal for Ecclesiastical Affairs, and empowered provincial governors to veto the appointments of parish priests. In 1874 a second series of May Laws provided for the confiscation of the endowments of dissident parish priests and the desposition and ultimate imprisonment of recusant bishops. For the Catholics Prussia became a police state. In the first four months of 1875, for example, 241 clergy and 136 editors were fined or imprisoned and over a thousand parishes were left without incumbents. The isolation of the Catholic population from the rest of the community became particularly apparent on such occasions as the *Kaiser's** birthday or Sedan Day, which were celebrated exclusively by the Protestants (**50**).

Relations with the Polish and Alsace-Lorraine minorities also worsened as a result of the *Kulturkampf*. The Prussian government viewed the Poles in the eastern provinces with a new intolerance, which merely strengthened Polish nationalism (**38, 70**). The attempt to introduce German into Polish primary schools in 1873 led to the growth of local peasant organisations, which sought both to protect Polish culture and prevent the ejection of Polish peasants from their farms by Germans. Similarly in Alsace-Lorraine the resentment caused by the clumsy attempts to Germanise the population was exacerbated by the *Kulturkampf* (**87, 88**).

Although there were isolated riots in the Rhineland and the eastern provinces, Windthorst discouraged extra-parliamentary opposition on the grounds that it would only afford the government fresh opportunities for attack. Consequently he did not support Felix von Loë's attempt to emulate Daniel O'Connell's successful campaign in Ireland in the 1820s, by setting up the Association of German Catholics, which was quickly broken up by the police. Windthorst's policy of urging Catholic voters to make the elections 'a great plebiscite' (**50**, p. 182) against Bismarck's policies was impressively rewarded in the *Reichstag* elections of 1874. The *Zentrum*, in alliance with the Danes, Poles and Alsatians, won 91 seats [**doc. 34**]. Within the *Reichstag* and the Prussian *Landtag* his tactics were less successful, as he failed to exploit effectively Conservative suspicions of Bismarck or to prod the Liberals into opposing the government on constitutional issues.

In the early seventies the *Kulturkampf* cemented the unity of the National Liberals and tightened the party's links with Bismarck. However, the crash of 1873 and the subsequent lengthy depression gradually began to create a new political and economic climate, which was eventually to transform domestic politics. As the champions of *laissez faire* the Liberals were made to bear responsibility for what various groups did not like about the contemporary world' (**61**, p. 144). They were thrown on the defensive by demands for a change in the government's economic policy. A potential Conservative-*Zentrum* economic consensus was beginning to emerge by 1876. The agrarian crisis reunited the Conservative Party and transformed it into a protectionist party with a natural reservoir of support amongst the Protestant peasantry (**52**) [**doc. 31**]. The *Zentrum* was also forced to abandon free trade under pressure from its voters, many of whom were small farmers and craftsmen who were particularly severely hit by the depression.

The collapse of the economic consensus and the emergence of parties based on sectional interests accelerated the decline of German Liberalism (**61**). Fundamentally both Liberal parties lacked the necessary constituency organisation and electoral base to compete successfully in a democratic franchise. They had at first profited from the low turnout in national and state elections, but their percentage of the vote steadily declined as the *Zentrum*, the Conservatives and later the *SPD* began to mobilise the hitherto apathetic masses (**56**). The impact of these external challenges was increased by the growing divisions within Liberalism. After Richter, who was a 'Progressive first and a Liberal second' (**61**, p. 138), became leader of his party in 1874, the differences between the two Liberal parties grew and by 1877 co-operation between them had virtually broken down. Simultaneously disagreements between the left and right wings of the National Liberal Party began to intensify.

The depression caused an acute crisis in the *Reich's* finances, the decline in industrial activity leading to a fall in the tax receipts of the individual states. This in turn undermined their ability to pay their regular matricular contributions to central government and was ultimately to check the expansion of the Imperial government's power at the expense of the states (**67**). The background of threatening international crisis in the Balkans made a solution to the financial problem even more urgent. Between 1875 and 1878 Bismarck considered ways of strengthening the *Reich's* finances and in the process became aware of the potential for fresh political alignments. Initially Bismarck had no overall plan and 'as so often in the critical moments of his career he experimented with several alternatives before settling on a definite course' (**93**, p. 194). He had hoped to tap new sources of revenue by nationalising the lucrative German railway companies, but he drew back in face of opposition from Bavaria, Saxony and Württemberg (**67**). The simplest solution was to increase indirect taxation on such articles as tobacco, sugar and brandy. However indirect taxation entailed a lessening of parliamentary control over the executive, since its payment became automatic once initial consent was granted, and both Liberal parties opposed it (**34**).

It is difficult to determine when Bismarck was converted to tariffs. In 1876 he discreetly began to encourage the protectionist campaign, but carefully avoided any commitment (**25**). It has been argued that he needed time to manoeuvre entrenched free-traders like Delbrück and Camphausen, the Prussian finance minister, out of their posts (**67**), but it is more likely that he was still keeping his options open [**doc. 37**]. However, both domestic and foreign pressures were nudging Bismarck into a decision against free trade. The protectionist campaign was gaining momentum (**80**) and privately Bleichröder informed Bismarck of the adverse effects of foreign competition on the Ruhr industries (**93**). Growing economic friction with Russia predisposed the government to protect German agriculture from Russian imports and made desirable closer diplomatic and commercial relations with protectionist Austria. This would be easier to achieve if Germany raised her tariffs to the Austrian level (**71**).

In late 1877 Bismarck attempted to win over the National Liberals to a programme of financial and constitutional reforms by offering Bennigsen the post of Prussian Minister of the Interior. However, they insisted that two further colleagues, who belonged to the left wing of the party (**25**), should also join the Cabinet. Their terms proved unacceptably high. The negotiations came to an end when Bismarck signalled his change of course by announcing in the *Reichstag* on 22 February 1878 the first stage of a comprehensive financial reform that would almost certainly involve the introduction of tariffs. It is possible (**32, 34**) that Bismarck was finally prompted into this decision by the election of Pope Leo XIII, who had indicated his desire for better relations with the *Reich*. However, although the prospects of gaining limited *Zentrum* support for tariffs may have been improved, it would be 'completely unrealistic' (**25**, p. 560) to argue that Bismarck was about to convert the *Zentrum* to a permanent ally. The wounds of the *Kulturkampf* were still too deep for that.

Having broken with the National Liberals, Bismarck had lost control of the *Reichstag*. In the spring of 1878, a majority for his finance legislation was uncertain. The first draft of the deputy bill was so emasculated that its main purpose of co-ordinating the *Reich* and Prussian governments was defeated (**25, 67**). The solution to Bismarck's problems lay in an early dissolution of the *Reichstag* and the election of a more manageable parliament in which a malleable National Liberal Party purged of its left wing would co-operate with a greatly strengthened Conservative Party [**doc. 38**]. On 11 May an attempted assassination of the *Kaiser*, at first erroneously thought to be a socialist plot, provided Bismarck with a chance to draft an anti-Socialist bill, that would not only strike at the fledgling *SPD* but also drive a further wedge between the two wings of the National Liberal Party. The bill was overwhelmingly defeated in the *Reichstag*, but a marvellously opportune second attempt on William's life in June enabled Bismarck to call a crisis election, in which the main thrust of his campaign was directed against the Progressives and left-wing National Liberals. Both Liberal parties were weakened and the Conservatives correspondingly strengthened, but the *Zentrum*, supported by the minor Nationalist groups, now held the balance in the *Reichstag* [**doc. 34**].

If Bismarck had been calculating that electoral defeat would bring the National Liberals to heel, their support for the second Anti-Socialist bill appeared to justify his tactics. In return for a concession which limited the law to an initial two-and-a-half-year period, the National Liberals joined the Conservatives and Free Conservatives in voting for the bill. It banned socialist meetings and publications and empowered the government to expel agitators from their homes [**doc. 39**]. The passage of the bill subjected the National Liberal Party to intense internal strain. The left wing, led by Lasker, was appalled by the right wing's delight in co-operating with the Conservatives. The right for its part was contemptuous of the left's reservations (**61**).

In the spring of 1879 Bismarck introduced legislation for levying tariffs on iron, iron goods and grain and for increasing indirect taxation on selected luxury goods. In a *Reichstag* of 397 members the support of the *Zentrum* bloc of 94 deputies was essential if the tariff bill was to pass. Windthorst supported protectionism for economic reasons but opposed indirect taxation if it enabled the government to evade financial control of the *Reichstag* and to weaken the power of the individual states. Bismarck sought to compel Windthorst's co-operation by negotiating directly with the Curia on alleviating the *Kulturkampf*, and to appease him by making minor concessions such as supporting the election of the *Zentrum* deputy, Baron von Frankenstein, as vice-president of the *Reichstag* and president of the tariff committee (**50**). Windthorst was, however, under considerable pressure from the *Zentrum* voters to demonstrate that support for protection did not entail general backing for Bismarck, who was still seen as the hated perpetrator of the *Kulturkampf*.

It soon became clear that Bismarck would have to choose between concessions to the *Zentrum* and to the National Liberals. Bennigsen, in a desperate attempt to preserve the unity of his party, agreed to support the bill provided the *Reichstag* could determine the salt tax and coffee duties annually, as well as two-thirds of the tariff income. Bismarck had no intention of strengthening parliament and probably only negotiated with Bennigsen to exert pressure on Windthorst (**50**). The bill's passage was finally assured when Bismarck accepted a *Zentrum* amendment, the *Clausula Frankenstein*. This strengthened the federal nature of the constitution by ensuring that only a fixed percentage of the income from the new duties and taxes would go directly to the central government and that the rest would be allocated annually to the states. The states would continue to make their annual matricular contribution to the *Reich* [**doc. 40**]. On 12 July 1879 a conservative, Free Conservative and *Zentrum* majority, joined by 15 right-wing National Liberal rebels, approved the bill.

The *Zentrum* had indeed made itself, as Windthorst was to observe, the liquidator of the 'bankruptcy of the Liberal economy' (**50**, p. 233) and enabled Bismarck to abandon free trade. The unity of the National Liberal Party was irreparably damaged. The 15 tariff rebels resigned, and the party became prey to bitter internal conflicts. These resulted in the secession of the left a year later. A foreign observer remarked that Bismarck had scored 'one of the most substantial triumphs of his political career' (**93**, p. 207), but, as the following decade was to show, Bismarck had in reality failed to solve any of the fundamental problems facing the *Reich*.

12 The Conservative Empire

It is usually argued that the changes in Bismarck's economic policy in 1878–79, and the subsequent political realignments, so transformed domestic politics that they resulted in what was in practice a second foundation of the *Reich* along more conservative lines (**49, 71**). Furthermore, Bismarck is held to have created a new alliance, composed of *Junkers*, *Zentrum* and heavy industry, as an authoritarian bulwark against the threatened encroachments of democracy (**64, 71**), to have transformed the parties into interest groups, and increasingly to have resorted to the Bonapartist tactics of plebiscitary elections and imperialist diversions. Obviously 1878–79 was an important turning point in both the domestic and foreign history of the *Reich*, but the transformation of German politics was not as comprehensive as is often depicted. Bismarck neither succeeded in making the *Reich* financially independent of the federal states (**67**) nor in persuading the *Zentrum* to join an anti-democratic *Sammlung** (**50**). His basic aim of adapting an essentially autocratic political structure to new socio-economic realities (**57**) could only be fleetingly achieved by employing one expedient after another. To defend the fragile structure of the Empire from revolutionary change became a 'labour of Sisyphus' (**141** p. 147) [**docs. 6, 37**].

For the National Liberals the upheavals of 1878–79 marked a traumatic turning point (**50, 61**). Bismarck's assumption that the party would split and that the rump would rally behind the government proved correct [**doc. 38**], but the divide fell nearer to the centre of the party than he had hoped. This delayed until 1887 the formation of an effective government bloc in the *Reichstag* (**25**). The National Liberals were barely able to fight the Prussian elections in 1879 as a united party, and in 1880 Lasker's resignation precipitated the secession of a further 27 deputies. In the *Reichstag* elections a year later Secessionist candidates won almost as many seats as the National Liberal Party itself. The character of the National Liberal Party changed as the traditional professional element was gradually replaced by businessmen and industrialists who favoured tariffs and co-operation with the Conservatives. The

Domestic Politics

drift rightwards was accelerated when the National Liberals in south Germany endorsed the Heidelberg Declaration in 1884. This unequivocally supported protection, approved of Bismarck's social insurance scheme and acknowledged the importance of agriculture in Germany's economic life.

The political realignments of 1878–80 greatly strengthened the position of the *Zentrum* in the Reichstag. Its vote for the tariff legislation of 1879 had demonstrated the value of its support for the government. In an attempt to ensure further co-operation, and thus a manageable parliament, Bismarck was ready to end the *Kulturkampf*, not by a premature capitulation to the *Zentrum* but on the basis of the new *status quo* created by the May Laws (**50**). Bismarck's initiatives for contrary reasons were viewed with suspicion by both the Catholics and the National Liberals. In July 1880 the discretionary relief bill, which would have empowered the government to suspend the May Laws on a selective basis, was amended when the Conservatives, prompted by the National Liberals, deleted a key provision enabling the government to pardon exiled prelates. Bismarck also tried to split the *Zentrum* by wooing its right wing. However Windthorst skilfully blocked any 'seepage on the right' (**50**, p. 301) by annually submitting to the *Landtag* a motion calling for the exemption of the administration of sacraments from criminal prosecution, which would have rendered the May Laws unenforceable. Its inevitable defeat by both the National Liberals and Conservatives enabled Windthorst to rally his party behind him and co-operate with the Progressives, who with the *Zentrum* had voted against the amended relief bill.

Bismarck suffered 'a sensational defeat' (**25**, p. 613) in the election of 1881 [**doc. 34**]. Over three-quarters of the *Reichstag* was now hostile to the government. Arguably (**61**) the voters were not so much rejecting Bismarck's reactionary politics as protesting against a sharp rise in retail prices and the financial effects of the tobacco monopoly. The Progressives and the Liberal Union (the former secessionists) won 106 seats between them. Even the *SPD* increased its number by 3 despite the anti-Socialist law and Stoecker's new Christian Social Party, which exploited anti-Semitism and promised a state welfare system (**56**).

The *SPD* had been severely affected by the anti-Socialist law. Although its deputies were not expelled from the *Reichstag*, its constituency organisation was broken up, the Labour press was virtually eliminated, socialist trade unions were dissolved and working-class clubs were dissolved. At a conference at Schloss

Wyden in Switzerland in 1880 the Party overwhelmingly decided to oppose the government by constitutional means and expelled the two principal exponents of political terrorism. The party adopted an organisational pattern that was 'informal, diffuse and often transitory' (**56**, p. 97). A new party paper, the *Sozialdemokrat*, was printed in Zürich and smuggled over the frontier by the 'red postmaster', Julius Motteler. Financial contributions were secretly collected, and an intelligence system was devised to counter the work of police informers (**51**). New electoral organisations, masquerading under the bland but legal name of 'societies for municipal elections', were created in the large cities, which enabled the *SPD* to rebuild its grass-roots organisation.

Confronted by an unruly *Reichstag* Bismarck openly talked of the possibility of a *coup d'état* (**63**) [**doc. 41**], as he had done in the early sixties. He purged the Prussian Cabinet, civil service [**doc. 42**] and the *Reich* Chancellor's office of liberally-inclined officials. He erected a further barrier against parliamentary control of the army by persuading William to allow the Military Cabinet and General Staff to report directly to the Emperor rather than to the War Minister (**34, 95**). In 1880 Bismarck took the first step in a plan, which drew its inspiration from Bonapartist France, for eventually neutralising parliament by setting up a Prussian Council on Political Economy in which representatives of 'the productive classes' of commerce, industry and agriculture would sit (**25**, p. 649, **71**). Bismarck viewed it as a prototype for a *Reich* Council and informed William candidly that he eventually intended to 'bypass' the *Reichstag* with it (**71**). When the scheme was debated it was overwhelmingly defeated by a *Zentrum* and Liberal majority. Bismarck's attempt to engineer a decrease in the number of parliamentary sittings by replacing annual with biennial budgets was also defeated in April 1881.

It has been argued that Bismarck's social welfare programme was another cynical manoeuvre 'to create in a new and strengthened form direct links with the state' (**25**, p. 604) and to woo the workers away from the *SPD*. Whether Bismarck 'in his own crude way . . . was not insensible to the sufferings of the poor' (**35 Vol. 2**, p. 38) is a matter for debate, but it is undeniable that the scale of his social legislation was at that time unique and 'enough to establish his reputation as a constructive statesman even if he had done nothing else' (**32**, p. 202).

The first accident insurance bill in March 1881 applied only to certain particularly dangerous industries. The employers were to pay two-thirds of the premiums, and the workers one-third, while the state was to supplement their contributions; but the National Liberals and the *Zentrum* combined to vote against the principle of state contribution, as the former suspected state socialism and the latter feared any strengthening of the central government. The bill also confronted the *SPD* with a dilemma. Either they had to accept economic amelioration at the hands of a suspect Bismarck or to adopt the ideological argument that genuine state socialism was only possible in a democratic society. A damaging split was avoided by the party's decision to propose amendments which the government would reject, thereby enabling the *SPD* to unite against the bill (**34, 56**).

After the elections of October 1881 Bismarck returned to his welfare programme. The *Reichstag* approved a health insurance scheme in May 1883 and an amended accident insurance bill in 1884, which was expanded to cover more industries without involving any financial contributions from the state. In both schemes Bismarck introduced a novel corporative element, which was in tune with his attempts to set up a *Reich* council on Political Economy (**38**). The health insurance scheme was partly based on the already existing organisation of miners' and crafts' guilds and was administered by local health committees which were elected jointly by employers and workers. The accident insurance scheme was run by the employers, who were organised in groups according to industries. Bismarck completed his welfare legislation with the introduction of the old-age pension in 1889. This was administered by the traditional bureaucracy both in Prussia and the other German states.

Besides attempting to tame the *Reichstag* through threatened *coups*, procedural reforms and the embryonic organisation of a corporate state (**63**), Bismarck continued to encourage a Conservative-National Liberal *Sammlung* and to woo the right wing of the *Zentrum*. In 1884 he attempted to split both the *Zentrum* and the new *Deutsche Freisinnige Partei**, which had been formed out of the two left-wing Liberal parties, by ostensibly seeking a renewal of the anti-Socialist law, but in reality hoping for its defeat so that he could prematurely dissolve parliament and fight the ensuing election on a programme which would expose their internal divisions. Bismarck was thwarted by a combination of right-wing *Zentrum* deputies and former Secessionists, whose vote just enabled the bill to pass. When the regular triennial *Reichstag* elections were held in the autumn, however, the *Freisinn*, penalised by middle-class voters for its official opposition to the bill and by working-class voters for the support which some of its rebels had given to the measure, lost nearly 40 seats (**50**). Although the Conservatives won 28, the National Liberals made only modest gains [**doc. 34**]. The *SPD* increased its seats to 24, which entitled it to regular representation on the *Reichstag* committees.

The underlying trend of the election results was distinctly encouraging for Bismarck. The 'nightmare' (**25** p. 655) of a large left-wing Liberal party receded and the dramatic rise in the socialist vote paradoxically facilitated the creation of a pro-government *Sammlung* in the *Reichstag*. His expansionary policy in Africa and South-East Asia gave the National Liberals a rallying cry and led to their close co-operation with the Free Conservatives on the colonial question (**61**). An increase in agrarian tariffs [**doc. 40**] and a bill aimed at buying out Polish farmers in the eastern provinces appeased the Conservatives. Nevertheless he was still confronted with an unmanageable *Reichstag* and was ready to exploit any further opportunity to dissolve at a favourable moment. He privately hoped for a socialist uprising, but the *SPD* stubbornly pursued a pragmatic and constitutional approach and no 'socialist gunmen' (**50**, p. 336) presented themselves as they had so conveniently in 1878.

It was the conjunction of the Bulgarian crisis with the rise of Boulanger in France in 1886 that finally gave Bismarck the chance to call an election under crisis conditions. Bismarck insisted on a 10 per cent increase in the size of the army and demanded a new *Septennat**, while the current one still had over a year to run. His intentions became clear when he dissolved the *Reichstag* in January 1887. This was in spite of a *Freisinn* motion for an immediate grant of the necessary funds for an initial period of three years, which the *Zentrum* was even willing to extend to five years (**50**), on the grounds that the issue at stake was not the length of the budget, but 'whether the Empire is to be protected by an imperial army or a parliamentary one' (**50**, p. 341).

The subsequent election [**doc. 34**] was fought in an atmosphere of artificially contrived crisis. The police vigorously enforced the anti-Socialist law and reservists were called up for manoeuvres in Alsace-Lorraine (**56**). The *Freisinn* and *SPD* each lost over half their strength, while the electoral *Kartell*, composed of the Conservatives, Free Conservatives and National Liberals, won 220 seats. Bismarck had at last engineered a majority, which passed the *Septennat* and enabled him, in March 1888, to meet with equanimity the accession of Frederick III, who died three months later of cancer (**65**). However, the *Kartell* was not an entirely reliable or subservient majority. There were tensions between the National Liberals and Conservatives which erupted in 1888 when the latter voted against further protective duties on wood and grain (**60**). Bismarck's reservations about the residual liberalism of the National Liberals were confirmed when Bennigsen demanded in 1889 the appointment of a *Reich* finance minister responsible to Parliament.

Bismarck did not exclude the possibility of eventual co-operation with the *Zentrum*. In 1885 he secured Papal support for the first 'Peace bill', which, despite some important concessions to the Catholics, still compelled the Church to register ecclesiastical appointments in Prussia with the provincial governors. Further concessions were made in the second 'Peace bill' in April 1887, which virtually ended the *Kulturkampf*. The right-wing of the *Zentrum* greeted it 'as the end of an unnatural 15 years of domestic exile'(**50**, p. 370) and welcomed the opportunity to work with the Conservatives. The first indication of a possible *rapprochement* came in mid-July 1889 when Bismarck raised no objection to the return of the Catholic Order of the Redemptionists to Bavaria.

The accession to the throne of the 29-year-old William II introduced a new political factor, which Bismarck consistently underestimated. William, flattered and encouraged by Field-Marshal von Waldersee and the leader of the National Liberals, Miquel, was determined not to be a mere figurehead. The court became a magnet for those officials and politicians who opposed Bismarck (**60**). On several key issues William found himself at loggerheads with his Chancellor. He agreed with Bismarck's critics in the Foreign Office on the allegedly dire consequences of ending the *Kulturkampf*, so far as internal developments in Bavaria and the future of the alliance with Italy were concerned. William was also critical of Bismarck's unrelenting hostility towards the *SPD* and consented to receive a delegation of miners during the strike in the Ruhr coalfields in 1889. He was also a keen supporter of the *Kartell* at a time when Bismarck was considering breaking with the National Liberals (**34**).

The events leading to Bismarck's resignation on 20 March 1890 have been obscured, partly by the nostalgia of German historians of the Weimar period who saw 1890 as the end of a golden age, and partly by Bismarck himself, who in retirement championed the cause of the *Kartell* parties and therefore hid his earlier disagreements with them (**60**). By the autumn of 1889 Bismarck had decided not to support the *Kartell* in the coming elections and instead to encourage a *Zentrum*-Conservative alliance since he increasingly disagreed with the National Liberals over a whole range of domestic and foreign issues. Röhl has argued that this sudden U-turn was intended to create 'a situation of such chaos . . . at home and abroad' that Bismarck, in the words of Holstein, a senior Foreign Office official, 'would have [had] the Kaiser in the palm of his hand' (**59 Vol. 1, 60**, p. 77). This is possibly an exaggerated view of his intentions (**50**), which reflects more accurately the strongly anti-Catholic views of the *Kaiser's* advisers. It is significant, for example, that when Bismarck started negotiations with Windthorst in March 1890, he took care to ensure that it would not endanger Germany's links with the anti-clerical Italian government. However it would be misleading to cast Bismarck in a moderate role in 1890. He was ready to risk confrontation with the *SPD* and to use the familiar scare of the 'red peril' as an election issue. This would also provide an excuse for a *coup* against the *Reichstag* if he failed to secure a *Zentrum*-Conservative *bloc*. Such a move would have created a far more apocalyptic scenario than an alliance with the *Zentrum* could ever have achieved.

In October Bismarck prepared a new anti-Socialist bill which was not only intended to operate permanently once it became law but also contained a draconian clause for the expulsion of socialist agitators. At the Crown Council meeting of 24 January 1890 Bismarck refused to modify the bill [**doc. 43**], and it was defeated in the *Reichstag* two days later. The *Kartell* broke up, and the subsequent election [**doc. 34**] in February led to a strengthening of the *Zentrum*, the *Freisinn* and the *SPD*. Having already broken with the *Kartell*, Bismarck's only options were to turn to the Conservatives and the *Zentrum* or to recommend a *coup*.

Bismarck and the *Kaiser* were set on mutually opposing courses. The *Kaiser* already had General von Caprivi waiting in the wings as the new Chancellor. Bismarck's former political expertise appeared to desert him when he clumsily tried to prevent William hosting an International Labour conference in Berlin and crudely enforced loyalty on his Prussian ministerial colleagues by resurrecting the Cabinet order of 1852, which restricted free access to the Crown to the Prime Minister. He also had contingency plans drawn up to deal with riots, which seemed to be more provocative than preventative (**29**). On 12 March 1890 Bismarck made his last serious attempt to stay in power when he approached Windthorst, but any hopes of a Conservative-*Zentrum* alliance were dashed when the leader of the Conservatives in the *Reichstag*, von Helldorf-Bedra, refused to co-operate and informed the *Kaiser* (**60**). On 17 March William finally demanded that Bismarck should either withdraw the Cabinet order of 1852 or resign. Isolated and defeated, Bismarck had little option but to resign the following day and on 29 March he left Berlin as a private citizen for his estate in Friedrichsruh. Ultimately, as the contemporary novelist Fontane observed, 'the power of the Hohenzollern monarchy ... was stronger than [Bismarck's] genius and his falsehoods' (**34**, p. 371).

Part Six: German Foreign and Colonial Policy

13 Germany and Europe, 1871–90 ·

As long as William I lived, German foreign policy was conducted by Bismarck alone. Although the quality of German diplomats was of the highest calibre, Bismarck's autocratic temperament in the long run served only to destroy their initiative (**34, 103, 148**) and consequently his diplomatic system remained 'a one man band' (**29**, p. 219). 1871 marks a natural turning point in his foreign policy: after three wars in a mere eight years there followed nearly twenty years of unbroken peace. Between 1862 and 1871 Bismarck had created a new Europe and, like Metternich in 1815, he now needed peace to preserve it.

The implications of France's defeat in 1871 were far reaching. Disraeli only slightly exaggerated contemporary fears when he observed that 'the war represents the German revolution . . . a greater event than the French Revolution of the last century' (**14**, p. 23). The military and diplomatic balance had shifted from Paris to Berlin and it was uncertain whether Bismarck would be able to contain the momentum of German nationalism within the frontiers of 1871. Yet the new Germany was still a 'delicate compromise' (**109**, p. 12) which could be destroyed by a hostile European coalition. Consequently Bismarck attempted to do 'everything to stave off the consequences of his own work' (**32**, p. 140) by assuring the great powers that Germany was 'saturated' and had no further territorial ambitions [**doc. 44**].

In the immediate post-war years Bismarck was primarily concerned to prolong French isolation. Both the severe terms of the Treaty of Frankfurt and the instability of internal French politics militated against an immediate military and economic revival. In the long term, however, a French recovery was inevitable. The League of the Three Emperors of Germany, Austria-Hungary and Russia in 1873 is sometimes seen as a premeditated attempt to isolate France (**24**), but initially it was more the product of mutual Austro-Russian distrust. Anxious to ensure that Vienna did not exploit her increasingly cordial relations with Berlin to Russia's disadvantage in the Balkans, Alexander 'gate-crashed' (**29**, p. 172) on Franz Joseph's visit to Germany in September 1872. In the subsequent hastily arranged tripartite talks Bismarck allayed Russia's suspicions and encouraged discussions on the maintenance of the *status quo* in the Balkans.

It was not until the following year, however, when a series of summits between the three Emperors produced the Agreements of 6 June and 22 October, that the League was finally created. Despite an accompanying Russo-German military pact, which Bismarck was careful not to endorse, it was essentially no more than an 'empty frame' (**109**, p. 30) in which the three powers stressed their desire for peace and agreed on mutual consultation before taking unilateral action in the event of war. Its conservative and anti-revolutionary bias has led to it being interpreted as 'a new Holy Alliance against revolution in all its forms' (**115**, p. 25), but it is more likely that Bismarck valued it chiefly as a means for isolating the French and enabling Germany to avoid making a choice between Russia and Austria. Arguably it initiated a policy which in varying degrees he attempted to follow until his resignation (**36**).

The League's limitations were first revealed by a sudden crisis with France in 1875. The speed with which the French had paid their indemnity and rebuilt their army alarmed the German government and persuaded Bismarck to resort to some crude sabre-rattling and to inspire a series of threatening articles in the German press. Amongst these was the notorious leader in the *Berliner Post* entitled 'Is War in Sight?' that suggested that he was about to launch a pre-emptive strike against France. Conscious that both Britain and Italy were equally alarmed, the Tsar visited William to express his concern, while Gorchakov, his Chancellor, demanded from Bismarck explicit assurances of peace. Although the crisis soon abated, Bismarck's miscalculations had enabled France to escape isolation and exposed the essential hollowness of the League of the Three Emperors (**109**).

Bismarck's diplomacy was subjected to a more testing challenge when the very existence of the Turkish Empire in Europe was threatened by a chain of events, beginning in July 1875 with uprisings in Bosnia and Herzegovina (**100, 115, 126**). A collapse of Turkish power in the Balkans threatened to create a vacuum which both Austria and Russia would compete to fill. At worst this threatened to lead to Austro-Russian conflict in which the rival powers would each seek a German alliance. At best a conference would be held where again the two powers would compete for German diplomatic support. In both situations Bismarck would be placed in essentially the same dilemma: he would be forced to chose between Vienna and St. Petersburg, with the consequence that the unsuccessful power would attribute its defeat to German intervention and so look towards France. Initially Bismarck attempted to reduce the growing tension between Russia and Austria-Hungary, whilst he avoided giving the Tsar the decisive backing he desired. Despite the brutal crushing of the Bulgarian revolt and the declaration of war on Turkey by Serbia and Montenegro, Russia and Austria-Hungary were still able to co-operate throughout the summer of 1876. At Reichstadt in July they drew up provisional plans for a peaceful partition of the Balkans. However, when Turkey, contrary to expectations, defeated both Serbia and Montenegro, Alexander came under increasing Pan Slav* pressure to intervene. In October he asked the German Government bluntly whether it would remain neutral in the event of war with Austria. Bismarck's reply was evasive and infuriated Gorchakov. He reiterated his hope for an Austro-Russian accord and stressed ambiguously that Germany could ill afford to see either empire permanently weakened.

The immediate threat of war abated when the great powers accepted a British proposal in November for an international conference to impose internal reforms on Turkey. When these were rejected by the Sultan in January 1877, Turkey was effectively isolated and, after talks in Budapest, Austria at last agreed in March to Russian intervention at the price of acquiring Bosnia and Herzegovina.

These developments did not prevent Russo-German relations during the winter of 1876–77 deteriorating to a point where the Prussian General Staff professed alarm at Russian troop movements in Poland. Bismarck, concerned by reports of a Russian diplomatic initiative in Paris, attempted both to exploit British suspicion of Russia's Balkan policy by proposing an Anglo-German alliance and to draw closer to Vienna. In November 1876 he told the Austro-Hungarian ambassador that any weakening of the Dual Monarchy 'would be contrary to German interests', and in February 1877, when London rejected an alliance, he added that he was considering a 'permanent organic link' between the two countries (**71**, pp. 495 and 443).

Although the coolness between Berlin and St. Petersburg partly reflected the personal animosity between Bismarck and Gorchakov and the Tsar's irritation that Germany had not proved a more reliable friend, it was also a result of fundamental changes in the social, economic and political structures of the two states. These were causing a growing friction that steadily exacerbated diplomatic differences (**71, 112**). As a consequence of the prolonged European depression, Russian industrialists, supported by Pan Slavs amongst the intelligentsia and in the Government, were becoming increasingly resentful of German economic penetration. They attempted to counter growing Russian dependence on German finance by urging their government to raise loans in Paris and to protect the Russian home market with high tariffs. The Government responded, and in 1877 the German export trade was severely damaged when Russian tariffs were abruptly raised by 50 per cent. This was followed by further increases of 10 per cent in both 1881 and 1884 (**112**).

Russia invaded Turkey in April 1877, but the Turkish force held out unexpectedly at Plevna and it was not until January 1878 that the Russians at last reached Constantinople. They then proceeded to negotiate a settlement that ignored the Budapest agreements and was consequently repudiated by both London and Vienna (**100**). To avoid a European war Bismarck had little option but to propose a congress in Berlin (**118**). Bismarck had hoped to deflect Russian hostility away from Austria and Germany towards Britain, but he failed, as his very neutrality and refusal to put pressure on Vienna was 'in essence a decisively anti-Russian act' (**126**, p. 248). This forced Russia to come to terms with Britain even before the Congress met. Although Russia made some very real gains at the congress, the partitioning of Bulgaria, which was interpreted as an attempt to hinder the spread of Russian influence in the Balkans, and the occupation of Cyprus and Bosnia and Herzegovina by Britain and Austria-Hungary respectively, gave rise to the bitter complaint in Russia that the congress had been 'a European coalition against Russia under the leadership of Prince Bismarck' (**34**, p. 113).

In the immediate aftermath of the congress Bismarck tried to revive the League of the Three Emperors, but by November it was clear that this was no longer possible. In the winter of 1878–79 he began to work towards an alliance with Austria-Hungary. Historians disagree about his motives. Some argue that Bismarck hoped to pacify Austria-Hungary and to compel 'Russia to adopt a more peaceful policy' (**128**, p. 250) and that consequently his emphasis on the organic character of the alliance [**doc. 45**] was merely 'an emotional coating' (**32**, p. 209) for home consumption.

On the other hand Langer, who described the alliance as 'the logical completion of German unification begun in the 1860's' (**115**, p. 196), and more recent German historians credit Bismarck with the much more fundamental aim of creating a Central European *bloc* or *Mitteleuropa*. This would both provide 'a sphere of influence for the commercial and political dynamism of the new Reich' (**71**, p. 591) and hold the balance between the emerging giants of Russia in the east and the British Empire in the west (**25**). The alliance was also potentially popular within Germany as it appealed to Catholics, National Liberals, Conservatives and the army. At a time of intense political divisions over tariffs, therefore, it can also be seen as a means for creating an 'internal consensus' (**25**, p. 595).

Emperor William remained stubbornly loyal to the Tsar and hostile to the Austrian alliance, but Bismarck's policy was facilitated by the increasing hostility of the Russian government. This was heightened by close Austro-German co-operation on the various technical commissions supervising the execution of the Berlin Treaty (**12**) and then further by the German tariff of July 1879 which discriminated against Russian grain imports. The German grain tariffs [**doc. 40**] were a particularly severe blow against the Russian economy. Over the next decade they did much to strengthen anti-German feeling at St. Petersburg. Three-quarters of all Russian exports were in corn, most of which went to Germany, and the profits played an important part in financing the industrialisation of Russia. This was crucial if Russia was to remain a great power, as the profits helped pay the interest on vital foreign loans.

In August the Tsar crudely attempted to bring Germany to heel by writing directly to William the so-called 'Box on the Ears Letter' in which he bluntly warned him of the consequences to Russo-German relations of Bismarck's policy. Chancellor and Emperor disagreed profoundly in their reaction. For Bismarck, acutely conscious that the pro-German Austrian foreign minister, Count Andrassy, was about to resign, it was the signal to accelerate negotiations with Austria. William, on the other hand, visited the Tsar in an attempt to lessen the tension. Fearful that William would surrender abjectly and commit Germany to an alliance with an unstable Russia, Bismarck, in a series of lengthy memoranda at the beginning of September, argued strongly that only an Austrian alliance could stabilise the Balkans, prevent the isolation of Germany, and compel Russia to agree to the re-creation of the Three Emperor's League. However, it was Bismarck's threatened resignation that finally persuaded William to sign the Austrian treaty on 7 October. The Dual Alliance was a 'landmark in European history' (**34**, p. 114), but it fell far short of Bismarck's original *bloc* concept and even failed to secure Austro-Hungarian support in the event of war with France. For an initial period of five years it provided that if either power were attacked by Russia, its ally would come to its assistance, but that if either partner were attacked by any other power, then its ally would observe benevolent neutrality (**115, 126**).

Even while Bismarck was concluding this alliance with Austria, he began to restore Germany's relations with Russia. Alexander, having failed to call Bismarck's bluff, indicated in late September 1879, when he sent Saburov to Berlin, that he desired a *rapprochement* with Germany and would even consider a new tripartite agreement involving Austria. The Saburov mission was a diplomatic victory for Bismarck as it vindicated his belief that Russian policy would become more flexible in response to a definite Austro-German alliance (**115**). Little progress could be made, however, until Austria was ready to give up the prospect of a British alliance. When Gladstone won the General Election in April 1880 and abandoned Disraeli's hawkish policy in the Balkans, the Austrians agreed to tripartite talks in Berlin in August 1880. Having guaranteed her empire against Russia, Bismarck could now afford to exert pressure on Austria to respond to Russian demands less negatively. In his desire to square the circle, however, he had to mislead the Russians into believing that the Dual Alliance did not entail the automatic defence of Austria-Hungary by Germany in the event of a Russian attack. The Three Emperors' Alliance was concluded initially for three years on 18 June 1881 (**119**) [**doc. 46**]. Although it was 'a hard-headed practical agreement' (**126**, p. 209), it was in many ways 'little more than an armistice' (**12**, p. 110) as it did not remove the long term causes of Austro-Russian rivalry in the Balkans. Austria conceded the eventual reunification of Bulgaria in exchange for the recognition of her right at some future date to annex outright Bosnia and Herzegovina. Russian security was strengthened by the reaffirmation of the closure of the Straits to warships, which effectively put the Black Sea beyond the range of the British navy. Bismarck was, at least temporarily, freed from the fear of a Franco-Russian treaty by the declaration that in the event of war with a fourth great power, the signatory powers would be bound to benevolent neutrality.

The Alliance of the Three Emperors did not lead to a stable

Russo-German *détente*. The humiliation of Russia at the Berlin Congress had the effect of 'unbalancing psychologically the designing of Russian foreign policy' (**112**, p. 417) and of strengthening Pan Slav influence. The young and inexperienced Alexander, who succeeded his father in 1881, received conflicting advice from his pro-German Foreign Minister, Giers, and such Pan Slav ministers as Katkov, Pobedonostev and Dmitri Tolstoy. He reacted to this by attempting to implement both viewpoints simultaneously. Giers was encouraged to seek close diplomatic co-operation with Berlin, while behind his back the nationalists and Pan Slavs in the Foreign Office and the Military High Command were permitted to intrigue in the Balkans and master-mind anti-German press campaigns. The increasing anti-German bias to Russian policy became apparent in December 1881 when the ardent Pan Slav Nikolai Obruchev was appointed to the General Staff and the construction of strategic military railways was begun in Russian Poland. In January 1882 Bismarck was particularly annoyed when the popular and charismatic General Skobelev addressed a meeting of Serbian students in Paris and described the Germans as the natural enemies of the Slavs (**112**).

To preserve the alliance Bismarck had both to deter Pan Slav hostility and encourage Giers at the Russian Foreign Office. Consequently when Italy, annoyed by the French occupation of Tunis, proposed an alliance with Austria, Bismarck seized on the chance to create a Triple Alliance which indirectly strengthened Austria. Superficially the terms favoured Italy, in that the Central Powers would assist her in the event of a French attack, while in return she would militarily support them only if attacked by two great powers. The real gain for Bismarck, however, was that Austria was freed from the fear of an Italian attack, should war break out with Russia. Austria's position was further consolidated by an alliance with Serbia in June 1882 and with Rumania in 1883, to which Germany also acceded, thereby forming 'a clear defensive alliance against Russia' (**126**). Simultaneously, however, Bismarck also attempted to mitigate the growing economic tension between Russia and Germany by refusing demands from both Junkers and industrialists for further tariff increases. Despite this there were large increases in 1885 and 1887 [**doc. 40**]. He also used Russian dependence on German capital as an inducement to secure a more co-operative policy and he facilitated the renewal of the Three Emperors' Alliance in March 1884 by persuading Bleichröder and other German financiers to subscribe to Russian loans floated on the Berlin capital market (**93, 122**).

The emergence of a moderate and peaceful bourgeois republic in France by 1877 had enabled Bismarck, contrary to his earlier fears, to concentrate on the 'Eastern Question' without any real danger from French revisionism. Bismarck had every interest in keeping France pacific and as early as 1878 he began to prepare the ground for a Franco-German *entente*. He supported French interests in Rumania, the Near East and North Africa and made no secret of his motives when he told the French Ambassador in 1880, 'I want you to turn your eyes from Metz and Strasburg by helping you to find satisfaction elsewhere' (**126**, p. 272). Bismarck was delighted to see the French 'scatter their energies in new areas while picking up new enemies on the way' (**93**, p. 330). He encouraged them to take Tunis and exploited their resentment of the British occupation of Egypt in 1882.

Although Bismarck's colonial policy was primarily motivated by commercial considerations (**133**), Taylor has argued that the German seizure of African colonies in 1884 was an attempt 'to make herself presentable to France [by] provok[ing] a quarrel with England so that Franco-German friendship should have the solid basis of anglophobia' (**137**, p. 18). It is argued in the next chapter that co-operation with France was a consequence rather than a cause of Bismarck's colonial policy (**139**), as for a brief period he genuinely needed French support against the British. Nevertheless it did provide him with opportunities to reinforce the general direction of his policy. In August 1884 he negotiated a Franco-German colonial *entente* and then co-operated closely with Paris in preparing the agenda for the Berlin Congo Conference. He surprised the French premier, Jules Ferry, with a proposal for an 'Association' of Continental powers as a 'counterweight to English colonial supremacy' (**140**, p. 385). He may have been momentarily reverting to his concept of a Continental *bloc* as a balance to the growing strength of the British Empire and Russia (**25**). The *entente* began to weaken as early as February 1885. The defeat of the moderate Republicans in the French elections effectively terminated Franco-German co-operation and led to the appointment as War Minister of the strongly anti-German General Boulanger in January 1886.

In September 1885 the Eastern Crisis again erupted when Bulgaria united under Prince Alexander of Battenberg. The Tsar now opposed unification as he feared the pro-British tendencies of the Prince. Initially the unity of the Three Emperors' Alliance was not threatened. Austria and Russia agreed on the necessity of restoring the *status quo*. Even when in the summer of 1886, after Serbia's failure to defeat Bulgaria, it became clear that this could not easily be achieved, Russian anger was principally directed against Britain. When Prince Alexander unexpectedly abdicated in September, Russia's attempts to reassert her influence in Bulgaria were viewed with growing suspicion by the Austrians who feared a Russian occupation of Bulgaria and the subsequent danger of a European war [**doc. 47**].

Although Bismarck exploited the rise of General Boulanger to fight a general election at a favourable moment, the conjunction of the Bulgarian crisis with the renewed threat from France was potentially dangerous. Bismarck was particularly concerned that Russian attempts to raise loans in Paris might lead ultimately to a Franco-Russian alliance (**93**). He 'manoeuvred desperately' (**112**), therefore, to preserve a link with Russia whilst simultaneously strengthening Austria-Hungary. He encouraged Britain, Italy and Austria-Hungary to conclude the first Mediterranean Agreement in February 1887 to contain Russia in the Balkans and at the Straits.

The Tsar refused to renew the Three Emperors' Alliance but agreed to negotiate with Germany alone what became known as the Reinsurance Treaty of 18 June 1887. Bismarck made considerable concessions, secretly acknowledging Russia's right to exert a dominant influence in Bulgaria and agreeing to the closure of the Straits to warships of all foreign powers. However, to maintain the Dual Alliance with Austria-Hungary he had to consent to a Russian proposal binding both signatories of the Reinsurance Treaty to neutrality in a war fought by the other with a third power, except in the situation where Germany attacked France or Russia attacked Austria. Bismarck had at least lessened the danger of a Franco-Russian alliance, but he had committed Germany to support Russia in Bulgaria in contradiction to Austria-Hungary's wishes, and consequently he ran the risk of encouraging the very war in the Balkans he wished to avert.

The pressure on Bismarck eased when Boulanger was dropped from the French Cabinet in May 1887, but the Reinsurance Treaty did not immediately lessen the tension in the Balkans. Russia viewed the election in July of Prince Ferdinand of Coburg to the Bulgarian throne as an Austrian conspiracy. Throughout the autumn the familiar manifestations of Russian displeasure with Germany were exhibited: there were fresh troop movements on the

Polish frontier and constant attacks on Bismarck in the press. Bismarck had initially been sympathetic to Russian protests, but he did not hesitate to use financial pressure to avert a Russian occupation of Bulgaria, even though in the longer term this would strengthen Russian financial ties with France. In November the German government effectively vetoed a loan to Russia when it ordered the *Reichsbank** not to accept Russian bonds as collateral security for loans. This led to a sudden collapse of confidence in Russian credit and a dramatic decline in the value of Russian securities held in Germany (**115**). In December Bismarck created a further bulwark against Russia when he successfully persuaded Britain, Austria and Italy to conclude the second Mediterranean Agreement, which aimed to preserve the *status quo* in the Near East.

Bismarck's complex financial and diplomatic moves restrained the Tsar from overt military action, but for the next two years Russia consistently attempted to undermine Ferdinand and to isolate Bulgaria. Russia also turned to the French money market where, in March 1890, a loan was so oversubscribed that she was able to finance large-scale and threatening military manoeuvres on the German, Austro-Hungarian and Rumanian frontiers (**115**). Paradoxically the accession of William II, who listened to the anti-Russian counsels of Waldersee and Holstein (**59 Vol. 1**) and showed a marked preference for a British alliance, made the Tsar more appreciative of Bismarck and anxious to renew the Reinsurance Treaty. Bismarck was ready to extend the treaty indefinitely, but he was dismissed in March 1890 before negotiations could begin. Convinced by Caprivi, Bismarck's successor, that a renewal would alienate Britain and contradict the spirit of the Triple Alliance, William allowed it to lapse in June and 'one of the pivotal agreements' (**115**, p. 503) of Bismarck's alliance system collapsed.

Reacting against Langer's famous encomium that 'no other statesman of (Bismarck's) standing had ever before shown the same great moderation and sound political sense of the possible and the desirable' (**115**, pp. 503–4), more sceptical historians have described his complex and contradictory alliance system as a 'conjuring trick' (**126**, p. 278), castigated it for 'expediency rather than creativity' (**34**, p. 102) and argued that the preservation of peace was in fact more a result of 'the good sense and moderation of others' (**128**, p. 254) than the inherent consequence of Bismarck's genius. Ultimately Bismarck's alliance system failed because it did not remove the basic causes of international instability. Bismarck had the 'simple and logical' (**112**, p. 421) aims of both preventing an Austro-Russian war and discouraging either power from allying with France against Germany. However, as this involved an assumption of permanent French isolation and of close co-operation between Vienna, St. Petersburg and Berlin, it was unsustainable in the long term. There was no guarantee that the multiracial and multilingual Austria-Hungary would not fragment and that Russian expansionism could indefinitely be kept in check. Bismarck's diplomacy was also becoming unpopular within Germany where economic differences with Russia and a hostile reaction against the anti-German bias of Pan Slav opinion made the doctrine of preventive war against Russia and co-operation with Austria-Hungary increasingly attractive (**60**).

14   The Creation of the German Colonial Empire

The haste with which Bismarck in 1884–85 created a colonial empire five times the size of the German *Reich* is one of the most controversial aspects of his Chancellorship. Up to that point he had always apparently dismissed colonial acquisitions as an expensive luxury comparable to 'a poverty stricken Polish nobleman providing himself with silks and sables when he needed shirts' (**138**, p. 160).

There have been attempts to resolve the problem, as Taylor does, by arguing that German colonies were 'the accidental by-product of an abortive Franco-German *entente*' (**137**, p. 6), or by casting Bismarck in the rôle of a crypto-imperialist, who since 1871 had patiently laid his plans for a colonial empire. Mary Townsend, for example, interprets the despatch of German consuls to Africa and the South Seas in the early seventies as evidence of 'cautious preparation and watchful waiting' (**138**, p. 62). Other historians argue that Bismarck's imperialism was principally motivated by short-term domestic objectives and that he played the colonial card in 1884 'like a magician producing a rabbit from a hat' (**34**, p. 167) to strengthen the appeal of the National Liberals in the autumn elections. It would be rash to deny that there was an element of opportunism in Bismarck's colonial policy. Thanks to the success of the *Kolonialverein** (founded in 1882 to promote colonial acquisitions), and the growing consensus of opinion among leading National Liberals that imperialism would help re-unite their party (**61**), the prospect of an active colonial policy was a potentially popular election cry (**141**). Conscious of the apparently imminent accession of the anglophile Crown Prince, Bismarck may also have favoured imperialism as an issue which could be exploited to produce an immediate quarrel with the British, should there be an attempt to dismiss him in favour of a 'German Gladstone ministry' (**24**, p. 274).

Such essentially opportunist interpretations are rejected by Wehler (**140, 141**), who describes Bismarck's colonial policy more as 'manipulated social imperialism', or a subtle attempt to guarantee continuous economic growth and social stability and 'to defend the traditional social and power structures of the Prussian state' by diverting attention away from divisive domestic problems (**141**, p. 153, **133**, p. 136) [**doc. 6**]. The very comprehensiveness of this view has led to further debate. Kennedy (**133**), drawing on a series of detailed studies (**132, 134, 139**) of Bismarck's colonial policy, argues that the concept of social imperialism, although relevant to the later Wilhelmine period, is not applicable to the eighties. He interprets Bismarck's policy rather as a pragmatic and limited response to pressure on German trade in Africa and the South Seas, and to his determination that Germans 'should not be pushed out of tropical markets where they had been operating for years at a time when industry and trade were already in the doldrums' (**133**, p. 139).

In the early eighties German merchants faced increasing competition in Africa and the Pacific. In New Guinea their interests were threatened by the territorial ambitions of the British Australian colony of Queensland, and the Cabinet in London had imperiously rejected a request for setting up a joint commission to review the claims of German merchants on the Fiji islands [**doc. 48**]. At the same time colonial trading companies in Hamburg and Bremen were pessimistic about their prospects in Africa. In the summer of 1883 Bismarck was so alarmed by reports that an Anglo-French partition of west Africa was imminent that he took the unusual step of consulting the Hamburg Chamber of Commerce, which confirmed his fears (**139**). Bismarck was persuaded in August to drop his lukewarm attitude towards the plans of F. L. Lüderitz, a Bremen tobacco merchant, for setting up a trading station on the south-west African coast at Angra Pequena, and not only to grant him consular protection but also to enquire whether Britain had any claims to the territory. It is possible that Bismarck had already decided on annexation, but he may have been hoping for written confirmation of British indifference so that he would be able to avoid the expense of a formal annexation (**139**).

It has been observed that 'in their almost incredible bungling born of complacency and arrogance, Lord Granville at the Foreign Office and Lord Derby at the Colonial Office must be regarded as the patron saints of Bismarck's empire' (**93**, p. 410). In November Bismarck was ambiguously informed that whilst Britain did not exercise sovereignty over the south-west African coast, she would regard it as an infringement of her 'legitimate rights' (**139**, p. 62) for another power to claim it. In December, when Bismarck sought clarification, he received no answer for six months. His suspicions were further aroused by the activities of local British officials at Cape Town and on the Gold Coast, who were pressing for the annexation of south-west Africa, Togoland and the Cameroons. German traders were also alarmed at the implications for the future of German trade in Central Africa when the Anglo-Portuguese Treaty of February 1884 allotted the mouth of the River Congo to Portugal, a power seen as a British satellite in Africa.

In the spring of 1884 Bismarck decided to grant formal protection not only to Lüderitz's acquisitions [**doc. 48**] but also to German trading interests in Togoland, the Cameroons and New Guinea, and he despatched plenipotentiaries to West Africa and the South Pacific to negotiate with the relevant local native chieftains (**139, 140**). Bismarck's reservations about the cost of colonies had been overcome by a formula devised by von Kusserow, a Foreign Office official, which by ceding responsibility for the internal administration of the territories to the trading companies themselves (**139**), would leave the *Reich* only with responsibility for external protection. The British were informed of the decision to protect Lüderitz in a cryptic note on 24 April, which Taylor interprets as a manoeuvre to goad Britain into opposition (**126, 137**). It is more likely to have been a deliberate attempt to mislead London so as to prevent any last minute effort to pre-empt German plans in south-west Africa and elsewhere (**139**). In retrospect this secrecy was justified, as the British did in fact send out an official to annex the Cameroons, who, unaware of rival German plans, arrived five days too late.

Bismarck took the obvious step of bringing pressure to bear on the British by exploiting Anglo-French differences in Egypt, and in August 1884 Germany ostentatiously supported France at the international conference on Egyptian finances in London. He also needed French support to counter Anglo-Portuguese policy in the Congo. When a blunt German refusal to recognise the validity of the Anglo-Portuguese Treaty of February 1884 led to the convocation of the Congo Conference in Berlin in December, Bismarck was particularly anxious to secure in advance French co-operation (**140**). Ironically, despite his repeated threats to organise a league of neutrals against Britain, a common desire to preserve free trade in the Congo led to an unexpected Anglo-German rapprochement and a corresponding weakening of the Franco-German *entente*. Bismarck was satisfied when the powers set up the Congo Free State under Belgian administration and stipulated that its frontiers were to remain open to international commerce.

Bismarck also hoped to strengthen German access to central African markets by negotiating with the Sultan of Zanzibar, who controlled an extensive stretch of the east African coast, a commercial treaty on such favourable terms that he would virtually become a client monarch of the *Kaiser*. This essentially diplomatic approach was threatened by the conquistatorial activities (**140**) of Carl Peters, the eccentric founder of the Society for German Colonization. Attempting to emulate the deeds of his heroes, Warren Hastings and Clive, he penetrated into the east African interior and rapidly concluded a series of treaties with the local chiefs by which he secured some 60,000 square miles of land. Rapidly transforming his Colonial Society into a trading company, he was able to persuade Bismarck of the commercial potential of the territory and gain Imperial protection in February 1885. The Sultan's objections to Peters' activities were overcome by a naval demonstration, and finally in December a commercial treaty covering the transit of goods through the Sultan's territory was signed.

Although Britain disliked Germany's colonial policy, she was distracted by French hostility in Egypt and Russian threats in Asia, and therefore had no choice but to tolerate it. In June 1884 the British Cabinet recognised the German *fait accompli* in south-west Africa and in October the protectorates in Togo and the Cameroons. In 1885 Britain abandoned her claims to north-eastern New Guinea and the adjacent islands of New Britain. By the Anglo-German agreement of October 1886 Britain finally recognised the German possessions in east Africa.

None of these territories was to prove profitable (**129, 135, 138**). Bismarck had hoped to create a colonial empire on the cheap, but having once intervened, the *Reich* was unable to extricate itself. In Togo and the Cameroons the *Reich* failed to devolve responsibility for internal administration to the local merchants and, where administrative responsibility was handed over to a chartered company, the experiment was short-lived. In 1888 the East African Company provoked a major native uprising (**140**), compelling Bismarck to send troops and partially to suspend its charter. Meanwhile the South-West African Company showed itself so incompetent that its powers were vested in an Imperial Commissioner (**138**), and in 1889 the New Guinea Company went bankrupt (**140**).

It is not surprising that Bismarck rapidly became disillusioned with colonies, as they proved to be a financial and administrative burden rather than a cheap means of guaranteeing a prosperous colonial trade. Apart from an unsuccessful attempt to strengthen the East African Company by acquiring the lease of some important coastal strips from Zanzibar in 1888, Bismarck sanctioned no further expansion. He showed no interest in plans for annexing Uganda and in early 1890 even favoured selling up German commercial interests in Samoa to the Americans (**134**). Increasingly he looked towards China and Latin America to provide potential export markets (**140**).

Bismarck's motives for this *volte face* are unclear. To historians (**137**) believing in the principle of the primacy of foreign policy in modern German history it is the natural consequence of the failure of the French *entente* and of Germany's need for British support during the Bulgarian crisis. The diplomatic situation certainly played some part, but it is probable that he was influenced at least as much by the financial failure of his colonial policy. Hence on pragmatic commercial grounds he became increasingly sceptical of the value of Germany's new colonies.

Part Seven: Assessment

15 Bismarck in Myth and Reality

Foreign observers in Berlin were surprised by the relief which greeted the news of Bismarck's resignation. The Austrian ambassador, for instance, recorded that the officials in the *Bundesrat* felt as if 'a heavy load has been taken away' (**159**, p. 310). By 1890 Bismarck appeared to have exhausted his genius for improvisation and to have 'had no other answer for the problems of his society but violence' (**34**, p. 179). His resignation was popular and regarded as inevitable, but within a year he became a considerable political force again when Caprivi, his successor, alienated both the Conservatives, by lowering agricultural tariffs, and the National Liberals, by the occasional tactical alliance with the *Zentrum*. Bismarck began to write scathingly critical articles for the *Hamburger Nachrichten* and was even elected as a National Liberal to the *Reichstag* although he never took up his seat.

In sharp contrast to his attitude between 1886 and 1890, when he rejected any further colonial acquisitions on the grounds that they were too expensive to maintain, he supported the imperialist and *Grossdeutsch* Pan-German League, which enabled his successors to claim Bismarckian authority for a German *Weltpolitik*. He also gave his blessing to the Agrarian League which was set up to oppose Caprivi's tariff policy and grew into a powerful pressure group, reinforcing Conservative determination to maintain the *status quo*. Bismarck's estate at Friedrichsruh became a mecca for students and representatives of various patriotic organisations, who were treated to lectures on the political blunders of his successors. By the time he died in 1898 the 'historical Bismarck' had already been eclipsed by 'the superhuman Bismarck, who from the Meuse to the Memel decorated market places and rural resorts in stone and bronze'. In retirement he had become 'an archetypal father figure and a national symbol' (**159**, p. 317), who lent his name to causes which, as Chancellor, he would have treated with greater circumspection.

However much the legacy left by Bismarck may tarnish his achievements in retrospect, his skill as a diplomat and politician cannot but impress the historian. He steered Prussia through the Schleswig-Holstein crisis, won the wars of 1866 and 1870–71 and negotiated the constitutional settlements of 1867–71. Undeniably the victory at *Königgratz* enabled Bismarck to end the constitutional crisis and to deflect the Liberal opposition. The constitutional settlements of 1867–71, however, were by no means a *diktat* and were real if fragile compromises between the Prussian Crown, the German states and the Liberal movement. For a decade after 1866 Bismarck enjoyed a creative alliance with the National Liberals, and although he continued to pay lip-service to the past, his policies were in practice more concerned with the future (**25**).

The constitution only remained viable as long as the majority of the *Reichstag* refrained from attacking the prerogatives of the Crown and Bismarck could reconcile the interests of Prussia with those of the *Reich*. This was the case during 'the golden age of the politics of compromise' (**76 Vol. 2**, p. 337) between 1867 and 1873. However, the prolonged economic depression and the rapid tempo of industrialisation in the 1880s changed the context of German politics. The introduction of tariffs in 1879 and Bismarck's subsequent alliance with the agrarians and industrialists sharpened class tensions and encouraged the growth of a strong *SPD*, which the anti-Socialist law was unable to prevent. Bismarck then employed every means he could to strengthen the executive and secure a pliant *Reichstag* (**49, 141**) [**doc. 6**]. Whether he can more accurately be compared to Napoleon III or Guizot is academic (**57**). Bismarck admired Napoleon's manipulation of the mass electorate and was skilful in seizing chances to hold elections at favourable opportunities, but by 1890 he was convinced that the constitution was unworkable and that it could only be revised by means of a *coup d'état*.

The interpretation of Bismarck's historical legacy remains one of the most crucial questions in German historiography. With superb skill Bismarck had constructed and manipulated the *Reich* constitution, but 'with the egoism that accompanies greatness' (**40**, p. 219) he failed to prepare any successor and 'no one, neither the erratic Kaiser William II nor the Chancellors who succeeded Bismarck – the well meaning Caprivi, the senile Hohenlohe, the pliant Bülow and the grey bureaucrat Bethmann Hollweg – could fill the gap' (**73**, p. 17). Yet even the most gifted statesman would have found the legacy difficult. The accelerating industrialisation of Germany created tensions which were virtually insoluble within the existing constitutional framework. Moreover the Prussian

Bismarck in Myth and Reality

agrarian military elite, strengthened by formidable peasant and artisan support (**73**), blocked any moves towards creating a parliamentary democracy, arguably the only solution which would in the long term have broken the domestic deadlock (**143**). Externally the problems were almost as intractable. Economic pressures were inexorably driving Russia into a French alliance and threatening to isolate Germany. Bismarck had no long-term solutions for the dilemmas facing the *Reich*. He had with increasing difficulty attempted to reconcile the Austrian alliance with continued links with Russia. Domestically his brilliant, but essentially negative, manipulation of the system provided only short-term expedients. To keep the Bismarckian constitution functioning the Prussian-German ruling elites were driven to employ ever more desperate measures. By 1914 they were ready to wage an offensive war in a Europe where, unlike the period 1856–71, the diplomatic balance no longer favoured Germany (**143**).

Part Eight: Documents

German historians

Eckart Kehr, 'the father of modern German historical revisionism' (79, Introd.), stressed that German historiography reflects the course of German history.

The task of analyzing the present state of German historiography is fraught with difficulty because it is so closely bound up with, and determined by, the general social and political development of the empire and the republic. Since the middle of the nineteenth century German historiography has been an almost perfect mirror image of the political-social situation. Speaking of one of the most famous works of German history, Mommsen's *Roman History*, which was honored with a Nobel Prize in 1902, fifty years after the first edition, the distinguished historian Eduard Meyer said that one could learn more from the book about German liberalism in the 1850's than about the whole history of Rome up to the death of Julius Caesar. The history of German historical writing is a part of general German History. It does not stand by itself, but touches at every point general social and internal relationships.

Kehr, (**152**), p. 174.

The Economy and National Unity

The Bremer Handelsblatt, a leading Liberal newspaper, stressed on 11 July 1857 the need for German unity. Its journalists were later active in the Nationalverein.

Whoever looks at the situation without prejudice and fear will recognize immediately the intimate connection, especially in Germany, of the national economic with the national political problem, this Alpha and Omega of German politics. The commerce and transportation of a country have, in spite of the egoism among individuals, a common aspect. They demand one law, one legislation, one defence abroad. This need has been satisfied in all other countries which we may mention, but not in Germany. A common code of commercial law is now slowly struggling to life; a common legislation is a pious wish, and abroad we all enjoy the same right, defencelessness. Now there are people who like, for example, the Geestemünde trade in its Geestemünde particularity as something specifically Hanoverian, and are able to close their eyes to the fact of its undeniable Weser nature. There are others who judge the transit tolls solely by whether their preservation is more advantageous to Stettin or their abolition more favorable to Hamburg. With people of such exceptional gifts and views we have nothing to do. The *Bremer Handelsblatt* has sought to represent the interests of German commerce and still seeks to do so. But we have something to say to and about such people.

Anderson, (**68**), p. 149.

document 3

The Nationalverein Programme, 1859

The League advocated the creation of a united Germany under Prussian leadership.

1 We perceive in the present political situation of the world great dangers for the independence of our German fatherland, dangers which have been increased rather than decreased by the peace concluded between Austria and France.
2 These dangers have their ultimate cause in the defective common constitution of Germany, and they can be removed only through a prompt alteration of this constitution.
3 For this purpose it is necessary that the German federal diet be replaced by a stable, strong, and permanent central government of Germany, and that a German national assembly be convoked.
4 Under present circumstances the most effective steps for the achievement of this goal can come only from Prussia. We should therefore strive to bring it about that Prussia assumes the initiative in this matter.
5 Should Germany in the immediate future once again be directly threatened from abroad, then, until the final establishment of the

German central government, the command of the German military forces and the diplomatic representation of Germany abroad are to be assigned to Prussia.

6 It is the duty of every German to support the Prussian government to the best of his ability, insofar as its endeavors are based on the principle that the tasks of the Prussian state coincide essentially with the needs and tasks of Germany, and insofar as it directs its activity toward the introduction of a strong and free common constitution for Germany.

7 We expect of all German friends of the fatherland, whether they belong to the democratic or the constitutional [right-wing liberal] party, that they will place national independence and unity above the demands of the party, and that they will work together harmoniously and perseveringly for the achievement of a strong constitution for Germany.

Hamerow, (**76 Vol. 1**), p. 316.

document 4

The Prussian Liberals long for a German Cavour

Karl Twesten in the Landtag *congratulated the Italians on achieving virtual unity, 1861.*

If some day a Prussian minister would step forward in the same way and say . . . 'I have moved boundary markers, violated international law, and torn up treaties, as Count Cavour has done,' gentlemen, I believe that we will then not condemn him. And if an inexorable fate should carry him off in the midst of his brilliant career, as happened to the former, before he achieved his high goal to its full extent, then we will erect a monument to him, as the history of Italy will erect one to Count Cavour, and I believe that even a soaring ambition will be content with such a monument.

Hamerow, (**76 Vol. 2**), p. 171.

document 5

King William and the army bill

The King contemptuously brushed aside an attempt by an old Liberal acquaintance, von Saucken Julienfelde, to explain the position of the Landtag *on the military question. In the extract from a letter below written in August 1862 'one can still hear the pen stab the paper and the ink explode' (**68**).*

War to the death against the monarch and his standing army has been vowed, and in order to reach that goal the Progressivists and democrats and ultra liberals scorn no means, and indeed with rare consequence and deep conviction . . . the shortening of the term of service is demanded so that firm, well disciplined military training, the effects of which will hold during the long period of leave, shall not be given the soldier. The under-officers shall become officers, not as everyone could in Prussia since 1808 by passing one and the same examination, but without proving this equality of cultural level, so that a schism will develop in the officers' corps and dissatisfaction will slowly creep into them and the democrats will be able to develop an officers' caste of their own which, because they are neither trained nor steeled in their views to stand loyally by the throne, are to be won for the revolution. Since loyalty and self-sacrifice for King and throne are to be expected from the present officers and through them to be transferred to the troops, *therefore* the officers' class is slandered in every possible way, and then one wonders that the officers are angry? And even censures them for this!!

'A peoples' army [behind] Parliament.' That is the solution revealed since Frankfurt am Main [he referred to a speech by Schulze-Delitzsch] to which I counter with the watchword:

'A disciplined army that is also the people in arms, [behind] the King and war lord.'

Between these two watchwords no agreement is possible.

Anderson, (**68**), pp. 106–7.

document 6

Hans-Ulrich Wehler's interpretation of Bismarck's politics after 1871

Bismarck's greater Prussian Imperial State, as founded in 1871, was the product of the 'revolution from above' in its military stage. The legitimacy of the young *Reich* had no generally accepted basis, nor was it founded upon a generally accepted code of basic political convictions, as was to be immediately demonstrated in the years of crisis after 1873. Bismarck had to cover up the social and political differences in the tension-ridden class society of his new Germany, and to this end he relied on a technique of negative integration. His method was to inflame the conflicts between those groups which were allegedly hostile to the *Reich*, *Reichsfeinde*, like the Socialists and Catholics, left-wing Liberals and Jews on the one hand, and those groups which were allegedly loyal to the Reich, the *Reichsfreunde**. It was thanks to the permanent conflict between these in- and out-groups that he was able to achieve variously composed majorities for his policies. The Chancellor was thus under constant pressure to provide rallying points for his *Reichspolitik*, and to legitimise his system by periodically producing fresh political successes. Within a typology of contemporary power structures in the second half of the nineteenth century Bismarck's régime can be classified as a Bonapartist dictatorship: a traditional, unstable social and political structure which found itself threatened by strong forces of social and political change, was to be defended and stabilized by diverting attention away from constitutional policy towards economic policy, away from the question of emancipation at home towards compensatory successes abroad; these ends were to be further achieved by undisguised repression as well as by limited concessions. In this way also the neo-absolutist, pseudo-constitutional dictatorship of the Chancellor could be maintained. By guaranteeing the bourgeoisie protection from the workers' demands for political and social emancipation in exchange for its own political abdication, the dictatorial executive gained a noteworthy degree of political independence *vis-à-vis* the component social groups and economic interests. And just as overseas expansion, motivated by domestic and economic considerations, had become an element of the political style of French Bonapartism, so Bismarck too, after a short period of consolidation in foreign affairs, saw the advantages of such expansion as an antidote to recurring economic setbacks and to the permanent direct or latent threat to the whole system and became the 'Caesarist statesman'.

Wehler, (**141**), pp. 122–3.

document 7
Bismarck foresees war with Austria

In April 1856 Bismarck sent Otto von Manteuffel and Leopold von Gerlach his assessment of Austro-Prussian relations.

Because of the policy of Vienna, Germany is clearly too small for us both; as long as an honourable arrangement concerning the influence of each cannot be concluded and carried out, we will both plough the same disputed acre, and Austria will remain the only state to whom we can permanently lose or from whom we can permanently gain . . . For a thousand years intermittently – and since Charles V, every century – the German dualism has regularly adjusted the reciprocal relations [of the powers] by a thorough internal war; and in this century also no other means than this can set the clock of evolution at the right hour . . . In the not too distant future we shall have to fight for our existence against Austria and . . . it is not within our power to avoid that, since the course of events in Germany has no other solution.

Craig, (**95**), p. 160.

document 8
Bismarck and the German Confederation

In March 1858 Bismarck wrote a lengthy memorandum for Prince William, which became known as the Booklet.

No state has the urge and opportunity to assert its German point of view independently of the *Bund** assembly to the same extent as Prussia, and it may at the same time prove that Prussia is of more importance to the middle and smaller states than a majority of nine votes for Prussia.

Prussian interests coincide exactly with those of most of the *Bund* countries except Austria, but not with those of the *Bund* governments, and there is nothing more German than the development of Prussia's particular interests, properly understood . . .

Medlicott and Coveney, (**12**), p. 21.

document 9
'Blood and Iron'

Bismarck's speech to the budget commission of the Prussian Landtag *on 29 September 1862.*

[He said] he would gladly agree to the budget for 1862, but without giving any prejudicial explanation. A misuse of constitutional powers could happen on any side, and would lead to a reaction from the other side. The crown, for example, could dissolve [parliament] a dozen times, and that would certainly be in accordance with the letter of the Constitution, but it would be a misuse.

In the same way it can challenge the budget cancellations as much as it likes: but the limit is difficult to set; shall it be at 6 million, or 16 million, or 60 million? – There are members of the National Union, a party respected because of the justice of its demands, highly esteemed members, who considered all standing armies superfluous. Now what if a national assembly were of this opinion! Wouldn't the government have to reject it? – People speak of the 'sobriety' of the Prussian people. Certainly the great independence of the individual makes it difficult in Prussia to rule with the constitution; in France it is different, the independence of the individual is lacking there. A constitutional crisis is not shameful, but honourable. Furthermore we are perhaps too 'educated' to put up with a constitution; we are too critical; the ability to judge government measures and bills of the National Assembly is too widespread; there are in the country too many subversive elements who have an interest in revolutionary change. This may sound paradoxical, but it goes to show how difficult it is in Prussia to carry on a constitutional existence . . . We are too ardent, we like to carry too heavy a weight of armour for our fragile bodies: but we should also make use of it. Germany doesn't look to Prussia's liberalism, but to its power: Bavaria, Wurttemberg, Baden can indulge in liberalism, but no one will expect them to undertake Prussia's role; Prussia must gather and consolidate her strength in readiness for the favourable moment, which has already been missed several times; Prussia's boundaries according to the Vienna treaties are not favourable to a healthy political life; not by means of speeches and majority verdicts will the great decisions of the time be made – that was the great mistake of 1848 and 1849 – but by iron and blood. . . .

Medlicott and Coveney, (**12**), pp. 30–1.

Bismarck and commercial reform, 1865

document 10

The Essen Chamber of Commerce in its annual report for 1865 approved of the new Prussian mining law which came into effect on 1 October 1865.

Unquestionably the most important event of the past year for our district was the coming into effect on October 1 of the 'General Mining Law for the Prussian States.' The new mining law marks the conclusion of a long period of striving for reforms and of their partial introduction. It completely removes everything antiquated and constraining, and instead gives mining the free movement which alone can make it great and beneficial. While the confusion in mining legislation was immeasurably increased by the vast number of laws and legal regulations which rested on the most diverse foundations and contained the most contradictory provisions, the new law on the other hand brings in clear and precise form a common standardization of the mining code, uniformly applicable to all mines in the state, which everywhere seeks to take into account the requirements of practical operation and the general legal views of the present time.

Hamerow, (**76(2)**), p. 221.

document 11

The internal impact of Düppel

In a letter to W. Rossmann (29 April 1864), J. G. Droysen, a distinguished historian and former Liberal deputy to the Frankfurt Assembly 1848–49 and one of the leaders of the Kleindeutsch *movement, confided his joy at the news of the military victory.*

I am certainly no Bismarck enthusiast, but he has the ability to act . . . I look forward to the future with pleasure. There is something invigorating, after fifty years of peace, in a day like the battle of Düppel for the young Prussian troops. One feels as if all one's nerves had been refreshed. And what a blessing that in the face of all the manoeuvring of the princes and the grandiloquence of the true Germans, the Austrian project for reform, and the *National-verein*, the full force of real power and real activism should make itself felt . . . It is time that the importance of the medium-sized and small states were kept within its real limits . . . They will go on saying that Prussia under Bismarck is not to be trusted; they will denounce more loudly than ever Prussia's greed for annexations and use it as a pretext for dissociating themselves; they will continue to say that the real Germany is outside Prussia and menaced by Prussia. With God's help all this will not stand in the way of what has been begun . . .

Simon, (**15**), p. 104.

document 12
Liberal opposition to the war of 1866

On 20 May a congress of Liberal deputies met in Frankfurt and condemned the imminent war with Austria.

The victory of our arms [over Denmark] has restored our northern boundaries to us. Such a victory would have elevated the national spirit in every well-ordered state. But in Prussia, through the disrespect shown for the rights of the reconquered provinces, through the effort of the Prussian government to annex them by force, and through the fatal jealousy of the two great powers, it has led to a conflict that reaches far beyond the original object of the dispute.

We condemn the imminent war as a cabinet enterprise, serving merely dynastic ends. It is unworthy of a civilized nation, threatens all achievements of fifty years of peace, and adds fuel to the greed of foreign countries.

Princes and ministers who will be responsible for this unnatural war, or who increase its dangers for the sake of special interests, will be guilty of a grave crime against the nation.

The curse, and the punishment for high treason, shall strike those who will give up German territory in their negotiations with foreign powers.

Bebel, (**17**), pp. 151–53.

document 13
Bismarck and Schleswig-Holstein

Bismarck indicated his thinking in the early stages of the Schleswig-Holstein crisis in a letter to the Prussian representative in Frankfurt on 22 December 1862.

I am certain of this, that the whole Danish business can be settled in a way desirable for us only by war. The occasion for such a war can be found at any moment that we find favorable for waging it. Until then, much more depends on the attitude of the non-German Great Powers towards the affair than on the intrigues of the Würzburg coalition governments and their influence on German sentiment. The disadvantage of having signed the London Protocol

[sic], we share with Austria and cannot free ourselves from the consequences of that signature without war. If war comes, however, the future territorial status of Denmark will depend upon its results.

It cannot be foreseen what development of German Federal relations is destined for the future; as long, however, as they remain about the same as in the past, I cannot regard it as in the interest of Prussia to wage a war in order, as the most favorable result, to install in Schleswig-Holstein a new Grand Duke, who in fear of Prussian lust for annexation, will vote against us in the Diet and whose government, in spite of the gratitude due to Prussia for its installation, will be a ready object of Austrian machination . . .

Steefel, (**124**), p. 52.

document 14
Bismarck defends the Austrian alliance, February 1865

Bismarck argued in a despatch to von der Goltz, the Prussian ambassador in Paris, that the Austrian alliance was worth preserving until circumstances changed.

I think it more useful to continue for a while the present marriage despite small domestic quarrels, and if a divorce becomes necessary, to take the prospects as they then prevail rather than to cut the bond now, with all the disadvantages of obvious perfidy, and without now having the certainty of finding better conditions in a new relationship later.

Stern, (**93**), p. 56.

document 15
Financing mobilization, July 1865

Von Roon informs Bismarck's old friend, Moritz von Blanckenburg, of the Government's success in raising money, 28 July 1865. Acting on Bleichröder's advice the Government sold its eventual rights to the ownership of the Cologne-Minden railway.

We have money, enough to give us a free hand in foreign policy, enough, if need be, to mobilize the whole army and to pay for an entire campaign. This gives our stance *vis à vis* Austria the necessary aplomb so that we may hope that they will give in to our

reasonable demands without war, which none of us wants . . .
Whence the money? Without violating a law, primarily through an
arrangement with the Cologne-Minden Railroad, which I and even
Bodelschwing consider very advantageous.

Stern, (**93**), p. 63.

document 16
The Gastein Convention, 14 August 1865

Article I   The exercise of the Rights acquired in common by the
High Contracting Parties, in virtue of Article III of the Vienna
Treaty of Peace of 30th October, 1864, shall, without prejudice to
the continuance of those rights of both Powers to the whole of both
Duchies, pass to His Majesty the Emperor of Austria as regards
the Duchy of Holstein, and to His Majesty the King of Prussia as
regards the Duchy of Schleswig.

Article II   The High Contracting Parties will propose to the Diet
the establishment of a German Fleet, and will fix upon the Harbour
of Kiel as a Federal Harbour for the said Fleet.

Until the resolutions of the Diet with respect to this proposal
have been carried into effect, the Ships of War of both Powers shall
use this Harbour, and the Command and the Police Duties within
it shall be exercised by Prussia . . .

Article III   The High Contracting Parties will propose in Frank-
fort the elevation of Rendsburg into a German Federal Fortress.
Until the Diet shall have issued the regulations respecting Garri-
soning the said Fortress, the Garrison shall consist of Imperial
Austrian and Royal Prussian troops under a command annually
alternating on the 1st July.

Article IV   While the division agreed upon in Article I of the
present Convention continues, the Royal Prussian Government
shall retain two Military Roads through Holstein; the one from
Lubeck to Kiel, the other from Hamburg to Rendsburg.

Article VI   [Provision for the duchies eventually to enter the
Zollverein.]

Article IX   His Majesty the Emperor of Austria cedes to His
Majesty the King of Prussia the Rights acquired in the aforemen-
tioned Vienna Treaty of Peace with respect to the Duchy of Lauenburg; and in return the Royal Prussian Government binds itself to
pay to the Austrian Government the sum of 2,500,000 Danish rix-
dolars, payable at Berlin in Prussian silver, 4 weeks after confir-

mation of the present Convention by their Majesties the Emperor
of Austria and the King of Prussia.

Article X ... The joint Command-in-Chief, hitherto existing,
shall be dissolved on the complete Evacuation of Holstein by the
Prussian troops and of Schleswig by the Austrian troops, by the
15th September, at the latest ...

[L.S.] G. Blome
[L.S.] von Bismarck

Medlicott and Coveney, (**12**), pp. 48–9.

document 17

Bismarck's peace policy, July 1866

*Bismarck describes in his memoirs the difficulties of convincing both the King
and the generals at Nikolsburg of the advantages of a moderate peace with
Austria.*

On 23 July, under the presidency of the King, a council of war was
held, in which the question to be decided was whether we should
make peace under the conditions offered or continue the war. A
painful illness from which I was suffering made it necessary that
the council should be held in my room. On this occasion I was the
only civilian in uniform. I declared it to be my conviction that
peace must be concluded on the Austrian terms, but remained
alone in my opinion; the King supported the military majority. My
nerves could not stand the strain which had been put upon them
day and night; I got up in silence, walked into my adjoining
bedchamber and was there overcome by a violent paroxysm of
tears. Meanwhile, I heard the council dispersing in the next room.
I thereupon set to work to commit to paper the reasons which in
my opinion spoke for the conclusion of peace; and begged the King,
in the event of his not accepting the advice for which I was responsible, to relieve me of my functions as minister if the war were
continued. With this document I set out on the following day to
explain it by word of mouth ...

We had to avoid wounding Austria too severely; we had to avoid
leaving behind in her any unnecessary bitterness of feeling or desire
for revenge; we ought rather to reserve the possibility of becoming
friends again with our adversary of the moment, and in any case
to regard the Austrian State as a piece on the European chessboard
and the renewal of friendly relations with her as a move open to

95

us. If Austria were severely injured, she would become the ally of France and of every other opponent of ours; she would even sacrifice her anti-Russian interests for the sake of revenge on Prussia.

Röhl, (**14**), pp. 20–1.

document 18
Russian and British views on Prussia's victory 1866

a) *On 6 October 1866 Lord Loftus, the British Ambassador in Berlin, informed Lord Stanley, the Foreign Minister, of the opinion of his Russian colleague at Berlin, d'Oubril.*

The former sympathy for Prussia appears to have returned, no expression of disapproval of Prussian annexation is heard. 'Les faits accomplis' no longer find a murmur. The only Legation of a neutral state which illuminated (altho' very modestly) on the eve of the entry of the victorious Prussian Army [into Berlin] was that of Russia. In short, the attitude of M d'Oubril is no longer one of jealous disquietude but has become one of passive and calm satisfaction.

b) *Lord Stanley viewed the future with some pessimism in a private letter to Lord Cowley, 18 August 1866.*

I begin to suspect that the German revolution may go farther and faster than its authors intend. Bismarck wants a new German federation. Napoleon wanted an Italian federation. We know what came of that: may not the precedent be followed? In any case the southern states will not long endure exclusion: and then will be seen, whether France and Russia will tolerate a German empire. But, as I think you said in one of your letters, it is a question for '68 rather than for '66.

Mosse, (**121**), pp. 248–9.

document 19
The National Liberals and the North German Confederation

a) *This letter by the Hanoverian Rudolf von Bennigsen, who was one of the founders of the* Nationalverein, *to A. L. Rochau, 29 December 1866, reveals* *that the National Liberals had realistic expectations of the North German Confederation.*

According to reports from Berlin very many conservatives will be elected [to the Constituent *Reichstag*] from the eastern provinces of Prussia, on the Rhine and in Westphalia allegedly a somewhat large number of ultramontanes. The physiognomy of the parliament will be extraordinarily different from that of 1848, and will play in terms of the standards of that time, a very modest role. If there is success, for which I do not despair, in organizing all north and central Germany with the help of parliament militarily and economically, and in these areas some emergency bridges are built to south Germany, a very firm basis for further development will have been achieved. The nation cannot ask for more at this time . . .

Windell, (**67**), p. 295.

b) *Bennigsen's colleague, Johannes von Miquel, was equally realistic in his electoral campaign address at Osnabrück, 1867, when he stated:*

The time of ideals is past. German unity has descended from the world of dreams into the prosaic world of reality. Politicians must ask today, not as before, what is desirable, but what is achievable.

Windell, (**67**), p. 295.

document 20

Bismarck on War, March 1867

Bismarck explains his attitude to the probability of a Franco-Prussian war to Count Bethusy-Huc, a Conservative Deputy in the Landtag.

Unhappily I believe in a war with France before long – her vanity, hurt by our victories, will drive her in that direction. Yet, since I do not know of any French or German interest requiring a resort to arms, I do not see it as certain. Only a country's most vital interests justify embarking on war – only its honour, which is not to be confused with so-called prestige. No statesman has a right to begin a war simply because, in his opinion, it is inevitable in a given period of time. If foreign ministers had followed their rulers and military commanders into the field, History would record fewer wars. On the battlefield – and, what is far worse, in the hospitals – I have seen the flower of our youth struck down by wounds and disease. From the window I can see many a cripple hobbling along the Wilhelmstrasse, looking up and thinking to himself if that man up there had not made that wicked war I would be at home strong and well. Such memories and sights would leave me without a moment's peace if I thought I had made the war from personal ambition or national vanity . . . You may rest assured that I shall never advise His Majesty to wage war unless the most vital interests of the Fatherland require it.

Palmer, (**29**), p. 133.

Bismarck and German Unity in 1869   document 21

In his famous dispatch to the Prussian Envoy in Munich in February 1869 Bismarck counsels patience until the circumstances favour action.

That German unity could be promoted by actions involving force I think is self-evident. But there is a quite different question, and that has to do with the precipitation of a powerful catastrophe and the responsibility of choosing the time for it. A voluntary intervention in the evolution of history, which is determined by purely subjective factors, results only in the shaking down of unripe fruit, and that German unity is no ripe fruit at this time leaps, in my opinion, to the eye. If the time that lies ahead works in the interest of unity as much as the period since the accession of Frederick the Great has done, and particularly the period since 1840, the year in which a national movement was perceptible for the first time since the war of liberation, then we can look to the future calmly and leave the rest to our successors. Behind the wordy restlessness with which people who do not know the trade search after the talisman that will supposedly produce German unity in a trice, there is generally hidden a superficial and, in any case, impotent lack of knowledge of real things and their consequences.

Craig, (**34**), p. 20.

document 22

The Ems Telegram

a) *Heinrich Abeken, a Prussian Foreign Office official, sent the following dispatch to Bismarck on 13 July 1870 at 3.40 p.m..*

His Majesty writes to me: 'Count Benedetti spoke to me on the promenade, in order to demand from me, finally in a very importunate manner, that I should authorise him to telegraph at once that I bound myself for all future time never again to give my consent if the Hohenzollerns should renew their candidature. I refused at last somewhat sternly, as it is neither right nor possible to undertake engagements of this kind *à tout jamais*. I told him that I had as yet received no news, and as he was earlier informed from Paris and Madrid than myself, he could see clearly that my government had no more interest in the matter.' His Majesty has since received a letter from Prince Charles Anthony. His Majesty, having told Count Benedetti that he was awaiting news from the Prince, has decided, with reference to the above demand, on the suggestion of Count Eulenberg and myself, not to receive Count Benedetti again, but only to let him be informed through an *aide-de-camp*: 'That his Majesty has now received from the Prince confirmation of the news which Benedetti had already received from Paris, and had nothing further to say to the ambassador.' His Majesty leaves it to your Excellency to decide whether Benedetti's fresh demand and its rejection should be at once communicated to both our ambassadors, to foreign nations, and to the Press.

b) *Bismarck edited it for publication as follows:*

After the news of the renunciation of the hereditary Prince of Hohenzollern had been officially communicated to the Imperial government of France by the Royal government of Spain, the French Ambassador further demanded of his Majesty, the King, at Ems, that he would authorise him to telegraph to Paris that his Majesty, the King, bound himself for all time never again to give his consent, should the Hohenzollerns renew their candidature. His Majesty, the King, thereupon decided not to receive the French Ambassador again, and sent the *aide-de-camp* on duty to tell him that his Majesty had nothing further to communicate to the ambassador.

Grant Robertson, (**26**), pp. 496–7.

document 23

French Partisans, December 1870

General Moltke described the threat posed by French partisans and the tactics taken to counter them in a letter to his brother, 12 December 1870.

The newly formed French armies have now all been gradually defeated on the open battlefield, but we are unable to be everywhere; minor ambushes cannot be prevented and are punished by pitiless severity. A handful of loafers singing the Marseillaise with guns and flags break into houses, shoot out of the windows and then run away out of the back doors, and then the town has to suffer for it. How lucky are those places which have a permanent enemy garrison in occupation . . .

von Moltke, (**21(2)**), p. 409 (translated).

document 24

Military impatience with Bismarck, December 1870

Lt. Col. Bronsart von Schellendorff, chief of operations in the General Staff of the Prussian army, 1870–71, records in his diary the army's irritation with Bismarck's determination to keep political control of the Franco-Prussian war.

(7 December 1870) Count Bismarck is really beginning to be fit for a lunatic asylum. He has complained bitterly to the King that General Moltke has written to General Trochu and maintains that, being a negotiation with a foreign government, this should fall into his own sphere of competence. But General Moltke, as a spokesman of the High Command, has written to the Governor of Paris; the matter is therefore a purely military one. Since Count Bismarck asserts further that he had stated to me that he regarded the letter as dubious, whereas the contrary is the case, I have immediately reported to General Moltke that the chancellor's statement is not true and have asked to be relieved in future of oral missions to him. The king, to whom General Moltke spoke about this matter, of course finds the whole thing very disagreeable, and the war minister said, very naively, that we ought not to pursue the matter too far, since in view of the diametrically opposed statements of my report and of Count Bismarck the only conclusion would be that one of us had been lying. General Moltke can hardly be in any doubt which one of us this was.

It is lamentable how inefficient our ministry of war is . . . General Roon is lazy . . . I have . . . shown that we must and can do more . . .

Simon, (15), p. 148.

Alsace-Lorraine

document 25

In 1891 Rémy de Gourmont dared criticise the French Government's refusal to accept the loss of Alsace-Lorraine. As a result he was dismissed from his job at the Bibliothèque Nationale.

Have they, in truth, become so unhappy, these corners of territory beyond the Vosges? Has one by chance made them change their language, their customs, their pleasures? . . . It seems to me that this has lasted long enough: this ridiculous image of the two little enslaved sisters, dressed in mourning and sunk to their knees before the frontier-post, weeping like heifers instead of tending their own cows. You may be sure that now, as before, they are gobbling their roasts with currant jelly, nibbling their salt pretzels, and guzzling their mugs of lager beer. Have no illusions: they are also making love and creating children. This new Babylonian captivity leaves me entirely cold.

Kennan, (112), p. 413.

Bismarck's power

document 26

The wife of the British ambassador, Lady Emily Russell, described in 1880 Bismarck's domination of the Emperor and the Government.

The *initiated* know that the emperor . . . has allowed Prince Bismarck to have his own way in *everything*; and the great chancellor revels in the absolute power he has acquired and does as he pleases. He lives in the country and governs the German Empire without even taking the trouble to consult the emperor about his plans, who only learns what is being done from the documents to which his signature is necessary, and which His Majesty signs without questions or hesitation. Never has a subject been granted so much irresponsible power from his sovereign, and never has a minister inspired a nation with more abject individual, as well as general, terror before. No wonder, then, that the crown prince should be worried at a state of things which he has not more personal power or influence to remedy than anyone else in Prussia, whilst Prince Bismarck lives and terrorises over Germany from Friedrichsruh with the emperor's tacit and cheerful consent.

Bismarck has gradually appointed a ministry of clerks out of the government offices, who do as they are told by him, and he has so terrified the *Bundesrat*, by threatening to resign whenever they disagreed with him, that they now vote entirely in obedience to his instructions. He now expects that at the next general election he will, by careful management, obtain the absolute majority he requires to carry through his new taxation and commercial policy.

If Bismarck should ever die suddenly from indigestion, which his doctors fear and predict, the difficulty of reforming the general abuses which his personal administration has created will be great, and will impose a hard and ungrateful task on the sovereign, who will have to find and appoint the ministers capable of re-establishing constitutionalism in Prussia.

Buckle, (**18 Vol. 3**), pp. 169–70

document 27

Speculation mania, 1871–73

A Berliner, Felix Philippi, described in his memoirs the frenzy of speculation on the Berlin Stock Exchange.

Everyone, everyone flew into the flame: the shrewd capitalist and the inexperienced petty bourgeois, the general and the waiter, the woman of the world, the poor piano teacher and the market woman; people speculated in porter's lodges and theatre cloak-rooms, in the studio of the artist and the quiet home of the scholar; the *Droschke** driver on his bench and Aujuste in the kitchen followed the rapid rise of the market with expertise and feverish interest. The market had bullish orgies; millions, coined right out of the ground, were won; national prosperity rose to apparently unimagined heights. A shower of gold rained down on the drunken city.

Craig, (**34**), p. 81.

The industrialisation of Germany

a) *Changes from rural to urban population*

	Total population	Per cent of population rural	Per cent of population urban*
1871	41,059,000	63.9	36.1
1880	45,234,000	58.6	41.4
1890	49,428,000	57.5	42.5
1900	56,367,000	45.6	54.4
1910	64,926,000	40.0	60.0

b) *Occupational distribution (in per cent)*

	1843	1882	1907
Agriculture and forestry	60.84–61.34	42.3	34.0
Industry and crafts	23.37	35.5	39.7
Commerce and communications	1.95	8.4	13.7
Public and private services	4.5–5.0	5.8	6.8
Domestic service	—	8.0	5.8

c) *Population growth of eight largest German cities*

City	1820	1870	1900	1910
Berlin	199,510	774,498	1,888,313	2,071,907
Breslau	78,930	207,997	428,517	517,367
Cologne	54,937	200,312	464,272	600,304
Essen	4,715	99,887	290,208	410,392
Frankfurt a.M.	41,458	126,095	314,026	414,576
Hamburg	127,985	308,446	721,744	953,103
Leipzig	37,375	177,818	519,726	644,644
Munich	62,290	440,886	659,392	665,266

Pinson, (**42**), pp. 221–22

* Urban = population of 2,000 or more.

document 29

The flight from the land

A British Royal Commission reporting on labour conditions in Central Europe in 1893 found that:

The general consensus of opinion in the country as a whole indicates a very great change for the better in the economic condition of the laborer during the last ten or twenty years. He is better fed and better clothed, better educated and better able to procure the means of recreation; nevertheless the migration statistics . . . indicate a continuous movement of the population from the agricultural east to the industrial west. Except in a few southern districts, such as Bavaria, where peculiar conditions prevail, the agrarian question proper, interpreted in Germany to mean the difficulty of procuring a sufficient supply of labor, scarcely exists in the west. With regard to the east, on the contrary, Dr Weber points out . . . that unless some means can be adopted for checking the outflow of the German population, there is every reason to fear that their places will be supplied by an inroad of Slavs, and that thus an element of disintegration already existing will be increased . . . The inquiry instituted . . . by the Economic Club (*Verein für Sozialpolitik*) has brought out clearly the predominant influence of the social over the economic factors in agrarian discontent. The gulf which separates the employer from the employed in the east, and the lack of opportunity for acquiring land are, in the opinion of the members of the Economic Club reporting on the subject, mainly responsible for its depopulation. Up to the present time it has appeared almost impossible to supply the remedy, though the great landowners are sufficiently ready to divide much of their land into small holdings, if this or any other measure would secure them a permanent supply of suitable labor.

Hamerow, (**9**), pp. 186–7.

Grain prices

The prices of wheat and rye in Berlin between 1871 and 1879 were:

Year	Wheat (marks per ton)	Rye (marks per ton)
1871	216	159
1872	238	163
1873	251	175
1874	233	170
1875	193	151
1876	206	154
1877	227	153
1878	194	132
1879	198	133

Lambi, (**80**), p. 133.

The foundation of the Association for the Reform of Taxation and Economy

One of the aims of the organisation was to consolidate the position of the Conservatives. This is emphasised by the following declaration which the constituent assembly of the Association accepted in February 1876.

In the field of economic and personal relations the absolute domination of Liberalism is to be broken and such institutions are to be formed which would be inspired by the conservative spirit and offer solid support to the Conservative Party.

The number of the followers of conservative principles is at present small. If we want to win over to conservatism wider circles, we must go along with the times. Indeed, we cannot betray our principles, but must at the same time follow the trends which move the people. We live in an era of material interests.

Lambi, (**80**), p. 138.

document 32
Grassroots support for protection

In February 1877 a small steering committee of Westphalian industrialists and agrarians met and drew up the following declaration which was then approved by an assembly of 400 representatives of Rhenish-Westphalian agriculture and industry on 10 March.

I In view of the impending renewal of commercial treaties and tariffs, the depression which has lasted for many years necessitates that agriculture and industry proceed in the future with the same solidarity which exists in reality without prejudicing individual political ties.

II For the promotion of general economic interests it is necessary:
a) to preserve and to develop home production as the first condition of general welfare;
b) the main factors for the attainment of this aim are low freight rates, well considered commercial treaties and tariffs, and a rational system of taxation, all based on actual conditions;
c) the discovery of the actual needs is to be reached through the questioning and consultation of experts;
d) the reform of the land and building tax and the mining tax which are to be covered through indirect taxation;
e) excepting the removal of direct and indirect export premiums enjoyed by foreign agricultural products, but which we spurn, German agriculture wants no further favours.

Lambi, (**80**), pp. 135–6.

document 33
Conditions of the urban working class in Germany, 1893

The British Royal Commission of 1893 provides accessible and invaluable data on the condition of the working classes and on the housing situation in the large cities. The continued migration of the rural population into the cities ensured housing shortages and high rents.

The Weaver's Budget given by Dr. von Schulze-Gaevernitz is as follows:

Weekly Budget of North German Weaver with Wife and four
Children

Income	M	Expenditure	M
Wages of father	15	42 lbs rye bread	
Amount paid by children		(second quality)	5.60
for board and lodging	7	30 pints potatoes	1.80
Total	22	2 lbs rolls	2.00
		2 lbs meal (second	
		quality)	0.40
		¾ lbs meat (Sunday)	
		½ suet	0.45
		vegetables	3.40
		coffee	0.20
		2½ lbs butter	3.40
		6 pints skimmed milk	0.60
		rent	3.20
		sick and old age	
		insurance	0.65
		school money	0.15
		Total	21.85

In Berlin the conditions are specially bad, and the average number
of persons inhabiting one tenement (*Grundstück*) has risen from 60.7
in 1880 to 66.0 in 1885. Subletting was shown by the census of 1880
to be exceedingly frequent, 7.1 per cent of the population took in
persons who boarded and lodged with them, and 15.3 per cent took
in persons to sleep (*Schlafleute*). One instance is given of a household
taking 34 such night lodgers, in another case there were eleven,
including two women. Thirty-eight per cent of the families taking
night lodgers lived in a single room; one instance is mentioned in
which a man and his wife with a family shared their one room with
seven men and one woman. Though the worst kind of night shel-
ters, known as 'Pennen', have now been suppressed by the police,
it is still 'the opinion of experienced observers . . . that the evils
existing in the large towns of England are less crying than in
Germany' . . .

The great lack of suitable dwellings for the working classes in the large towns of Germany, the degree of overcrowding that exists, and the heavy rents, which must be paid, have been illustrated by a series of tables compiled by Herr Trüdinger, of the Tübingen University.

Character of dwellings in six of the large cities of Germany

City	Year	Number of Dwellings	Proportion per 1,000 with the Possibility of Heating				Proportion per 1,000 Situated in			
			No rooms	One room	Two rooms	More than two rooms	Cellars	Ground floor	Attics	Other floors
Berlin	1880	255,929	13	498	265	224	91	146	163	589
Hamburg	1880	88,826	10	393	284	300	65	204	55	546
Breslau	1880	60,615	6	590	217	187	41	132	122	688
Dresden	1880	49,833	2	593	204	241	29	148	170	604
Leipzig	1880	28,510	1	285	272	442	20	157	135	682
Frankfurt am Main	1880	27,763	1	236	222	541	1	174	43	715

Proportion of the Population Living under the above Conditions

City	Year	Proportion per 1,000 Inhabitants Living in Dwellings Situated in				Proportion per 1,000 Dwellings		Average number of Inhabitants in Dwellings, with Possibility of Heating		
		Cellars	Ground floor	Attics	Other floors	Small	Of these very over-crowded	No rooms	One room	Two rooms
Berlin	1880	92	148	155	587	776	115	3.1	3.7	4.5
Hamburg	1880	61	194	54	402	687	107	3.5	3.7	4.5
Breslau	1880	38	128	111	698	813	144	3.5	3.8	4.4
Dresden	1880	27	147	168	578	756	125	2.2	3.6	4.4
Leipzig	1880	17	151	145	673	558	–	2.4	3.8	5.1
Frankfurt am Main	1880	1	167	36	692	459	27	2.4	3.5	4.3

Hamerow, (**9**), pp. 180–2.

Reichstag Elections 1871–1912

PARTY	1871		1874		1877	
	No. Votes	No. Deputies	No. Votes	No. Deputies	No. Votes	No. Deputies
No. eligible voters	7,975,750		8,523,446		8,943,028	
No. valid votes cast	4,134,299	397	5,259,155	397	5,535,785	397
Conservatives	548,877	57	359,959	22	526,039	40
Reichspartei[†]	627,229	67	431,376	36	426,637	38
National Liberals	1,171,807	125	1,542,501	155	1,469,527	128
Progressives	361,150	47	469,277	50	597,529	52
Center	724,179	63	1,445,948	91	1,341,295	93
Poles	176,072	13	199,273	14	219,159	14
Social Democrats	123,975	2	351,952	9	493,288	12
Guelphs	60,858	7	92,080	4	96,335	4
Danes	18,221	1	19,856	1	17,277	1
Alsace-Lorraine	234,545	15	234,545	15	199,976	15
Antisemites	. . . . .	. .	. . . . .	. .	. . . . .	. .
Other parties	66,670	. .	36,636	. .	14,153	. .

[†] Until 1871 the Free Conservatives

PARTY	1878		1881	
	No. Votes	No. Deputies	No. Votes	No. Deputies
No. eligible voters	9,124,311		9,088,792	
No. valid votes cast	5,811,159	397	5,301,242	397
Conservatives	749,494	59	830,807	50
Reichspartei	785,855	57	379,347	28
National Liberals	1,330,643	99	746,575	47
Progressives	607,339	39	1,181,865	115[†]
Center	1,328,073	94	1,182,873	100

[†] Includes 46 seats of the Liberal Union and 9 of the *Volkspartei*

Table continued

PARTY	1878		1881	
	No. Votes	No. Deputies	No. Votes	No. Deputies
Poles	210,062	14	194,894	18
Social Democrats	437,158	9	311,961	12
Guelphs	102,574	10	86,704	10
Danes	16,145	1	14,398	2
Alsace-Lorraine	178,883	15	152,991	15
Antisemites	. . . . . .	. .	. . . . . .	. .
Other parties	14,721	. .	13,010	. .

PARTY	1884		1887	
	No. Votes	No. Deputies	No. Votes	No. Deputies
No. eligible voters	9,383,074		9,769,802	
No. valid votes cast	5,811,973	397	7,527,601	397
Conservatives	861,063	78	1,147,200	80
Reichspartei	387,687	28	736,389	41
National Liberals	997,033	51	1,677,979	99
Progressives[†]	1,092,895	74	1,061,922	32
Center	1,282,006	99	1,516,222	98
Poles	206,346	16	221,825	13
Social Democrats	549,990	24	763,128	11
Guelphs	96,400	11	112,800	4
Danes	14,400	1	12,360	1
Alsace-Lorraine	165,600	15	233,685	15
Antisemites	. . . . . .	. .	11,496	1
Other parties	12,700	. .	47,600	2

[†] Between 1884 and 1893 the *Freisinnige Partei*

PARTY	1890		1893		1898	
	No. Votes	No. Deputies	No. Votes	No. Deputies	No. Votes	No. Deputies
No. eligible voters	10,145,877		10,628,292		11,441,094	
No. valid votes cast	7,298,010	397	7,673,973	397	7,752,693	397
Conservatives	895,103	73	1,038,353	72	859,222	56
Reichspartei	482,314	20	438,435	28	343,642	23
National Liberals	1,177,807	42	996,980	53	971,302	46
Progressives	1,307,485	76	1,091,677	48	862,524	49
Center	1,342,113	106	1,468,501	96	1,455,139	102
Poles	246,800	16	229,531	19	244,128	14
Social Democrats	1,427,298	35	1,786,738	44	2,107,076	56
Guelphs	112,100	11	101,800	7	105,200	9
Danes	13,700	1	14,400	1	15,400	1
Alsace-Lorraine	101,156	10	114,700	8	107,400	10
Antisemites	47,500	5	263,861	16	284,250	13
Other parties	74,600	2	129,000	5	397,500	18

PARTY	1903		1907		1912	
	No. Votes	No. Deputies	No. Votes	No. Deputies	No. Votes	No. Deputies
No. eligible voters	12,531,210		13,352,880		14,441,436	
No. valid votes cast	9,495,586	397	11,262,829	397	12,207,529	397
Conservatives	948,448	54	1,060,209	60	1,126,270	43
Reichspartei	333,404	21	471,863	24	367,156	14
National Liberals	1,317,401	51	1,637,581	54	1,662,670	45
Progressives	872,653	36	1,233,933	49	1,497,041	42
Center	1,875,273	100	2,179,743	105	1,996,843	91
Poles	347,784	16	453,858	20	441,644	18
Social Democrats	3,010,771	81	3,259,029	43	4,250,401	110

Table continued

PARTY	1903		1907		1912	
	No. Votes	No. Deputies	No. Votes	No. Deputies	No. Votes	No. Deputies
Guelphs	94,252	6	78,232	1	84,618	5
Danes	14,843	1	15,425	1	17,289	1
Alsace-Lorraine	101,921	9	103,626	7	162,007	9
Antisemites	244,543	11	248,534	16	104,538	3
Other parties	267,142	11	319,574	14	497,252	16

Pinson, (**42**), pp. 572–3.

document 35

Annual earnings of workers in industries, commerce and transport, 1871–1913

Year	Average annual income before deductions (tax, etc.) (in Marks)	Cost of living index (1895 = 100)	Average annual income after deductions (in Marks)
1871	493	105.8	466
1875	651	112.7	578
1880	545	104.0	524
1885	581	98.6	589
1890	650	102.2	636
1895	665	100.0	665
1900	784	106.4	737
1905	849	112.4	755
1910	979	124.2	789
1913	1083	129.8	834

Stürmer, (**47**), p. 41.

document 36

Bismarck attacks the Catholic Clergy

During the debate on the school supervision bill in the Prussian Landtag *on 10 February 1872 Bismarck made the following attack on the Roman Catholic clergy in Germany:*

The government cannot avoid the remarkable observation that the Roman Catholic clergy is national in all other lands. Only Germany makes an exception. The Polish clergy adhere to the Polish national movement, the Italian to the Italian . . . Only in Germany is there the peculiar phenomenon that the *clergy* has a more *international* character . . . The Catholic Church, even when she obstructs the development of Germany for the sake of foreign nations, is closer to its heart than the development of the German Empire . . . (Windthorst: 'Proof!') I cannot find an insult in that. (Call from the *Zentrum* and Right: 'Proof!') *Ach*, gentlemen, search your own hearts. (Long, lasting laughter.)

Anderson, (**50**), p. 159.

document 37
Bismarck's guiding principle in domestic policy

In 1881 he told the Reichstag:

I have often acted hastily and without reflection, but when I had time to think I have always asked: what is useful, effective, right, for my fatherland, for my dynasty – so long as I was merely in Prussia – and now for the German nation? I have never been a doctrinaire . . . Liberal, reactionary, conservative – those I confess seem to me luxuries . . . Give me a strong German state, and then ask me whether it should have more or less liberal furnishings, and you'll find that I answer: Yes, I've no fixed opinions, make proposals, and you won't meet any objections of principle from me. Many roads lead to Rome. Sometimes one must rule liberally, and sometimes dictatorially, there are no eternal rules . . . My aim from the first moment of my public activity has been the creation and consolidation of Germany, and if you can show a single moment when I deviated from that magnetic needle, you may perhaps prove that I went wrong, but never that I lost sight of the national aim for a moment.

Taylor, (**32**), p. 138 (Arrow Books, 1961).

The National Liberals and Bismarck

Notes for a political speech by Rudolf Haym, circa *February 1881:*

I take as my point of departure the conviction that the policy of
Prince Bismarck continues to centre on the national idea, and that
anyone who is as imbued with this idea as he is can gain an influence on this policy. I am convinced that the national idea cannot
and may not be separated from justified liberal demands. I am
convinced that even Prince Bismarck's vigilant foreign policy is
rendered more difficult if domestically he finds only enemies or only
majorities casually patched together from varying elements. I am
convinced that those aspects of his policy that I myself regard as
errors have been only stratagems which he was forced to employ
by the confusion among the parties. Some [parties] were more
conservative than national, others not national at all but only
clerical, yet others more liberal than national.

It is otherwise with us [National Liberals]. As the name of our
party deliberately indicates, we are prompted by the idea that
national and liberal interests affect each other reciprocally. For my
part I have no hesitation in saying that if on any specific issues the
liberal and the national interest should come into conflict I should
give the latter priority before the former. Liberal institutions, in my
view, are merely means to the end of attaining power for the state
and the best possible well-being for the individual ... We must
strive for as much freedom as the national state can tolerate; we
must impose on our striving for progress whatever limits the maintenance and consolidation of this national state demand. By and
large, Prince Bismarck represents for me the incarnation of the
national state. I do not always like his methods. Sometimes – I
have in mind particularly universal and equal suffrage – he has
gone too far in the direction of liberalism for my taste, at other
times he has regrettable tendencies and sympathies towards
conservatism, at yet other times he encourages interest-group
politics which appeals to egoism and therefore slights the nobler
motives in political life and must have a confusing and even
corrupting effect. But in the face of all this I remind myself that
nobody else has such a lively regard for the idea of making the
young empire vital, permanent, and resilient, and that he is untir-
ingly and successfully at work to realise this idea with sensible
realism according to circumstances. All his twists and turns and

inconsistencies can be explained by the power of this idea. Seen in this light, all the tortuous and often contradictory methods that he employs *vis-à-vis* the domestic factions, even his reckless experiments, become intelligible . . .

Simon, (**15**), pp. 221–2.

document 39

Extracts from the anti-Socialist law, 1878

1 Societies which aim at the overthrow of the existing political or social order through social democratic, socialistic, or communistic endeavors are to be prohibited.

This applies also to societies in which social democratic, socialistic, or communistic endeavors aiming at the overthrow of the existing political or social order are manifested in a manner dangerous to the public peace, and particularly to the harmony among the classes of the population.

Associations of every kind are the same as societies . . .

4 The (police) is empowered:

1 To attend all sessions and meetings of the society.

2 To call and conduct membership assemblies.

3 To inspect the books, papers and cash assets, as well as to demand information about the affairs of the society.

4 To forbid the carrying out of resolutions which are apt to further the endeavors described in 1, par. 2.

5 To transfer to qualified persons the duties of the officers or other leading organs of the society.

6 To take charge of and manage the funds . . .

28 For districts or localities where the public safety is menaced by the endeavors described in 1, par. 2, the following regulations may be decreed, in case they are not already permitted by state law, with the consent of the *Bundesrat* for a period not exceeding one year:

1 that meetings may take place only after the consent of the police authority has been obtained; this limitation does not extend to meetings called for the purposes of an announced election to the *Reichstag* or to the diets of the states;

2 that the distribution of publications shall not take place on public roads, streets, squares, or other public places;

3 that the residence in districts or localities of persons from

Documents

whom danger to public safety and order is to be feared may be
forbidden;
4 that the possession, bearing, importation, and sale of weapons
is to be forbidden, limited, or made conditional upon certain
requirements.
The Reichstag must be informed immediately, that is, upon its first
reassembling, about any decree that has been issued under the fore-
going provisions.
The decrees are to be announced in the *Reichsanzeiger** and by
whatever manner is prescribed for local police orders.
Whoever, knowingly or after public notice is given, acts in
contravention of these regulations, or of the decisions based
thereon, is to be punished by fine not exceeding one thousand
marks, or with arrest or imprisonment not exceeding six months.

Lidtke, (**56**), pp. 339–48.

German grain tariffs

document 40

Tariffs were levied as follows:

| Product | | Year | |
| | 1879 | 1885 | 1887 |
		(*Marks per ton*)	
Wheat	10	30	50
Rye	10	30	50
Barley	5	15	25
Oats	10	15	40
Flour	20	75	105

Lambi, (**80**), p. 230.

Rumours of a coup

document 41

Professor Mosler, who was on the left wing of the Zentrum, *wrote in
February 1886 'in strictest confidence to a friend' that*:

Evil things are in the works. The recent threats of a *Staatsstreich**
are meant seriously. If Bismarck does not get his Socialist Law and

116

the whisky monopoly, he wants to dissolve the *Reichstag* and impose a new imperial constitution, whereby the *Reichstag would result from the elections of the individual Landtage*. With that, of course, he would be rid of the *Zentrum* and the *Freisinn* completely and in one blow. This person is, as you know, capable of anything – so I do not consider even this plan impossible.

Anderson, (**50**), p. 335.

document 42
The Conservative bias of the Prussian Civil Service in the 1880s

Albert von Puttkammer, the son of Robert von Puttkammer, the Prussian Minister of the Interior, who purged the Prussian administration of Liberals, paints what Kehr describes as 'a pretty picture of this neofeudal bureaucracy' (79, p. 119).

The nobility formed the nucleus of the Conservative party, and in keeping with its tradition, insisted on a considerable measure of loyalty to the king. The whole younger generation of public servants was impregnated with these views. Bourgeois elements vied with their aristocratic colleagues in openly displaying their convictions. Anyone familiar with personnel conditions in Prussian government offices must know that liberal political views had almost no exponents among government officials. The younger generation was conservative in its political views.

Kehr, (**79**), p. 119.

document 43
Disagreement between William II and Bismarck, January 1890

Bismarck and William disagreed on the importance of the deportation clause in the new anti-Socialist bill which was being debated by the Reichstag.

His Majesty was pleased to accede to the proposal of the secretary of state for the interior . . . that the *Reichstag* should be dissolved after tomorrow's debate on the third reading of the Socialist Law and to declare his intention of performing the dissolution himself. With respect to the decision of the *Reichstag* on this bill His Majesty was pleased to remark that the power of deportation was scarcely of so far-reaching an importance as to jeopardize the passage of the bill in case of its rejection. It was undesirable to close this *Reichstag*, which had performed much useful work, in disharmony, which might, moreover, have an unfavourable effect on the elections and on the maintenance of the *Kartell*. Perhaps it was possible to postpone a consideration of this question for the future.

The ministers having been asked for their individual views, the prime minister declared to begin with that it was scarcely possible any longer to secure the agreement of the federated governments to forgoing a part of the bill laid before the *Reichstag* and that moreover he would emphatically advise against taking any such step which would be the first step down the road of concessions. Such a step would be calculated to damage the prestige of the governments and to weaken their position. The Socialist Law contained the minimum that the governments required in the way of the use of force. Probably more would have to be asked for later. This possibility was precluded if it was now conceded that one could do with less. Even in the expected new strikes in the coal districts the power of deporting the agitators out of this area would be very useful. According to his political experience he assumed that it would have an undesirable effect on the elections if the law was defective owing to faults *committed by the governments*. The maintenance of the *Kartell* would not be endangered if the law was rejected.

Simon, (**15**), p. 226.

document 44
Bismarck declares Germany a satiated power

Bismarck's conversation in 1871 with the British ambassador in Berlin was reported to London as follows:

In the first instance he wished to solicit my co-operation in contradicting calumny. It had been reported to him that the Queen of Holland who, for incomprehensible reasons of her own, was a bitter enemy of Prussia and of German unity, had succeeded during her frequent visits to England in propagating the idea that Prussia sought to annex the Netherlands with a view to acquiring colonies and a fleet for Germany, and Her Majesty had even persuaded Monsieur Rouher to commit himself to the statement that Germany wanted the Zuider Sea. This idea was utterly unfounded. No

German government could ever desire, nor would public opinion ever consent to the annexation of the Netherlands to the German Empire. Germany had long struggled for national unity and now that it was happily established, he thought forty millions of united Germans were sufficient to maintain the national independence they had acquired without having to resort to the conquest of peaceful industrious and friendly neighbors like the Dutch.

He neither desired colonies or fleets for Germany. Colonies in his opinion would only be a cause of weakness, because colonies could only be defended by powerful fleets, and Germany's geographical position did not necessitate her development into a first-class maritime power. A fleet was sufficient for Germany that could cope with fleets like those of Austria, Egypt, Holland, and perhaps Italy, scarcely with that of Russia, but it could not be a German interest so long as she had no colonies to rivalise with maritime powers like England, America, or France. Many colonies had been offered to him, he had rejected them and wished only for coaling stations acquired by treaty from other nations.

Germany was now large enough and strong enough in his opinion, and even the Emperor William's insatiable desire for more territory had not led him to covet the possession of the Netherlands.

He had had trouble & vexation enough to combat the Emperor's desire to annex the German provinces of Austria, the population of which certainly desired to form part of the great German family, but that desire he would oppose so long as he was in power, because he preferred the alliance and friendship of Austria to the annexation of provinces that would add nothing to the strength and security of Germany and the loss of which would lessen the value of Austria as an ally.

The Swiss, for instance, were a German-speaking nation, but Switzerland was of greater value as an independent friendly neighbor to Germany than as a province of the German Empire.

Hamerow, (**9**), pp. 142–3.

document 45

Bismarck defends the Dual Alliance

I was compelled by the threatening letter of the Czar Alexander to take decisive measures for the defence and preservation of our independence of Russia. An alliance with Russia was popular with nearly all parties, with the Conservatives from an historical tradition, the entire consonance of which with the point of view of a modern Conservative group is perhaps doubtful. The fact, however, is that the majority of Prussian Conservatives regard alliance with Austria as congruous with their tendencies, and did so none the less when there existed a sort of temporary rivalry in Liberalism between the two governments. The Conservative halo of the Austrian name outweighed with most of the members of this group the advances, partly out of date, partly recent, made in the region of Liberalism, and the occasional leaning to *rapprochements* with the Western Powers, and especially with France. The considerations of expediency which commended to Catholics an alliance with the preponderant Catholic Great Power came nearer home. In a league having the form and force of a treaty between the new German Empire and Austria, the National-Liberal party discerned a way of approximating to the quadrature of the political circle of 1848, by evading the difficulties which stood in the way of the complete unification, not only of Austria and Prussia-Germany, but also of the several constituents of the Austro-Hungarian Empire. Thus, outside of the social democratic party, whose approval was not to be had for any policy whatever which the government might adopt, there was in parliamentary quarters no opposition to the alliance with Austria, and much partiality for it.

Reflections and Reminiscences, (**3**, vol. 2), pp. 255–7.

document 46
Separate Protocol to the Three Emperors' Convention, 18 June 1881

1 Bosnia and Herzegovina.
Austria-Hungary reserves the right to annex these provinces at whatever moment she shall judge opportune.
2 Sandjak of Novibazar.
The Declaration exchanged between the Austro-Hungarian Plenipotentiaries and the Russian Plenipotentiaries at the Congress of Berlin under date of July 13/1 1878 remains in force. [The Russians recognised it as an Austrian sphere of influence.]
3 Eastern Rumelia.
The three Powers agree in regarding the eventuality of an occupation either of Eastern Rumelia or of the Balkans as full of perils for the general peace. In case this should occur, they will employ

their efforts to dissuade the *Porte* from such an enterprise, it being well understood that Bulgaria and Eastern Rumelia on their part are to abstain from provoking the *Porte* by attacks emanating from their territories against the other provinces of the Ottoman Empire.
4 Bulgaria.
The three Powers will not oppose the eventual reunion of Bulgaria and Eastern Rumelia within the territorial limits assigned to them by the Treaty of Berlin, if this question should come up by the force of circumstances. They agree to dissuade the Bulgarians from all aggression against the neighbouring provinces, particularly Macedonia, and to inform them that in such a case they would be acting at their own risk and peril.
5 Attitude of Agents in the East.
In order to avoid collisions of interests in the local questions which may arise, the three Courts will furnish their representatives and agents in the Orient with a general instruction, directing them to endeavour to smooth out their divergences by friendly explanations between themselves in each special case; and, in the cases where they do not succeed in doing so, to refer the matters to their Governments.
6 The present Protocol forms an integral part of the secret Treaty signed on this day at Berlin, and shall have the same force and validity . . .

(L.S.) Bismarck
(L.S.) Széchényi
(L.S.) Sabouroff

Medlicott and Coveney, (**12**), pp. 128–9.

document 47

The atmosphere at St. Petersburg, autumn, 1886

Bernhard von Bülow, the German chargé d'affaires in Russia, described in a private letter of 15 November 1886 how the Russian Government felt itself humiliated in Bulgaria.

Russia feels that she has disgraced herself without measure in Bulgaria. What has happened there in the last year – the Revolution in Philippopolis, Slivnica, Battenberg's return after the conspiracy of August 21, the manner in which he then abdicated, the behavior of the Regency, etc., – is viewed here as a series of humiliations. The sense of having produced this fiasco by one's own awkwardness only increases the touchiness. Vorontsov, on reading in the club an article about Kaulbars in the *Kölnische Zeitung*, remarked, with a bitter face: 'Nous sommes comme les chiens qu'on frotte avec le nez dans les ordures qu'ils ont faites.' The 'intelligentsia' is exasperated because the Panslav idea, which for twenty-five years has been regarded as an irreversible dogma, has turned out to be a great humbug . . . The Emperor is embittered because even after the removal of his arch-enemy Battenberg, things are going contrary to his expectations and wishes. Russia and the Tsar, in this mood, ask themselves on whom they should vent their wrath. On Bulgaria? The Panslavs warn against an occupation of Bulgaria, in which they see a mouse trap. On England? They would like to settle their scores with England only after Austria has been disposed of. On us? To be sure, we are hated here, and the Russians are not to be trusted. But this hatred flows more from a vague antipathy to what Germany represents than from political calculation. 'C'est plutôt par sentiment que par raisons politiques qu'on est chez nous contre les Allemands,' is what they often say. On the other hand the Russians, thank God, fear us greatly. An early attack on us is unlikely. This of course does not exclude spurring the French on behind the scenes. I have already, in August, drawn attention to the intrigues of Zagulyayev[1], Katakazi[2], etc. These semi-official approaches will probably continue. The immediate object of Russian anger is Austria. I hear from every side: 'Il faut déplacer la question bulgare.' That means that Russia should extract herself from the Bulgarian swamp by a confrontation with Austria.

1 An *attaché* at the Russian embassy at Paris
2 Probably a Russian journalist in Paris

Kennan, (**112**), pp. 213–4.

document 48

Angra Pequena

Bismarck announced the establishment of a Protectorate over Angra Pequena in a speech to the Budget Commission of the Reichstag, *23 June 1884.*

[Bismarck said that the Emperor would probably issue a *Schutzbrief*, similar to a British Royal Charter.] It might perhaps involve the

Documents

setting up of coaling stations and an extension of the consular system. These arrangements might eventually be used for other undertakings on the coast of Africa and the Pacific.

His earlier confidence that German undertakings would feel sufficiently safe under English protection was shaken, not *vis-à-vis* the British government, but by the behaviour of English colonial governments. He reminded them for instance that it had been necessary to remonstrate for years at the want of respect for the rights acquired by German landowners on the Fiji islands before the British occupation. And recently the Australian colonial governments had not only made excessive claims to independent territories in the Pacific, but had also proclaimed the principle that acquisitions of land in these regions which were made before an eventual occupation should be declared null and void.

If it were asked what means the German *Reich* possessed for protecting German undertakings in far-off places, the answer first and foremost would be the desire and interest of other powers to preserve friendly relations with her. If in foreign countries they recognized the firm resolve of the German nation to protect every German with the device *civis romanus sum*, it would not cost much effort to afford this protection. But of course if other countries were to see us disunited, then we should accomplish nothing and it would be better to give up the idea of overseas expansion . . .

Medlicott and Coveney, (**12**), p. 142.

Glossary

Bund The German Confederation

Cortes The Spanish Parliament

Deutsche Freisinnige Partei (Freisinn) The German Free Thought Party

Droschke cab

Grossdeutschland A united Germany including the German-speaking countries of the Austrian Empire

Gründerjahre The years when the *Reich* was established

Junker Prussian nobleman and landowner

Kaiser Emperor

Kartell Cartel or manufacturers' association to control production. Also an alliance of political parties

Kleindeutschland A united Germany without Austria

Kolonialverein Colonial Association

Kulturkampf A struggle between cultures

Landtag The Prussian Chamber of Deputies

Liberum veto The right to veto

Nationalverein The National Association

Pan Slav Initially a programme based on the brotherhood of equal Slav nations, and then increasingly synonomous with Greater Russian nationalism

Reich The Empire or state after 1871

Reichsanzeiger The official *Reich* gazette

Reichsbank The National Bank

Reichsfeinde Enemies of the State

Reichsfreunde Friends of the State

Sammlung A concentration or coalition

Septennat A septennial military budget

SPD (Sozialdemokratische Partei Deutschlands) German Social Democratic Party

Staatsstreich A *coup d'état*

Ultramontane Favourable to the absolute authority of the Pope

Wilhelmsstrasse The German equivalent to Whitehall

Zentrum Centre Party

Zollverein Customs Union

Bibliography

DOCUMENTS

Bismarck: letters, speeches, writings, etc.

1 Littlefield, W. (ed.) *Bismarck's letters to his wife from the seat of war, 1870–71*, Appleton and Co., 1903.
2 Andreas, W. and Reinkug, K. F. (eds.) *Bismarcks Gespräche von der Entlassung bis zum Tode*, Schünemann, 1963.
3 *Bismarck, the Man and Statesman, being the reflections and reminiscences of Otto Prince von Bismarck*, 2 vols, (trans. A. J. Butler), Smith Elder, 1898.
4 *Bismarck, Werke im Auswahl*, 8 vols, Kohlhammer, 1962–83.
5 Penzler, J. (ed.) *Correspondence of William I and Bismarck with other letters*, 2 vols (trans. J. A. Ford), Heinemann, 1903.
6 Petersdorff, H. von et al (eds.) *Die Gesammelten Werke Bismarcks*, 15 vols, Stollberg, 1924–32.

General collections

7 Bonnin, G. (ed.) *Bismarck and the Hohenzollern Candidature for the Throne of Spain*, Chatto and Windus, 1957.
8 'Bismarck's relations with England, 1871–1914', *German Diplomatic Documents, 1871–1914*, vol I, (trans. E. T. S. Dugdale) Methuen, 1926.
9 Hamerow, T. S. (ed.) *The Age of Bismarck. Documents and Interpretations*, Harper Row, 1973.
10 Hoefle, K. H. (ed.) *Geist und Gesellschaft der Bismarckzeit*, Musterschmidt, 1967.
11 Lepsius, J. et al (ed.) *Die Grosse Politik der Europäischen Kabinette, 1871–1914*, Deutsche Verlagsgesellschaft fur Politik und Geschichte, 1922.

Bibliography

12 Medlicott, W. N. and Coveney, D. K. (eds.) *Bismarck and Europe*, Edward Arnold, 1971.

13 Rich, N. and Fischer, M. (eds.) *The Holstein Papers*, 4 vols, Cambridge University Press, 1955–63.

14 Roehl, J. C. (ed.) *From Bismarck to Hitler. The Problem of Continuity in German History*, Longman, 1970.

15 Simon, W. M. (ed.) *Germany in the Age of Bismarck*, Allen and Unwin, 1968.

16 Snyder, L. L. (ed.) *Documents of German History*, Greenwood Press Publishers, 1958.

DIARIES AND MEMOIRS

17 *Bebel's Reminiscences*, Socialist Literature Company, New York, 1911.

18 Buckle, G. E. (ed.) *The Letters of Queen Victoria*, Second Series, 3 vols, Longman, Green and Co. 1926–30.

19 Knaplund, P. (ed.) *Letters from the Berlin Embassy, 1871–74*, U.S.G.P.O. 1944.

20 Loftus, Lord Augustus, *Diplomatic Reminiscences*, 4 vols, Cassell, 1894.

21 Andreas, W. (ed.) *Moltkes Briefe*, 2 vols, Bibliographisches Institut, Leipzig, 1922.

BIOGRAPHICAL STUDIES OF BISMARCK

22 Crankshaw, E. *Bismarck*, Macmillan, 1981.

23 Darmstaedter, F. *Bismarck and the Creation of the Second Reich*, Methuen, 1948.

24 Eyck, E. *Bismarck and the German Empire*, (trans. and abridged), Allen and Unwin, 1950.

25 Gall, L. *Bismarck – Der Weisse Revolutionär*, Propyläen, 1980 (trans. by J. A. Underwood, *Bismarck – The White Revolutionary*, Allen and Unwin, 1986).

26 Grant Robertson, C. *Bismarck*, Constable, 1918.

27 Headlam, J. *Bismarck and the Foundation of the German Empire*, Knickerbocker Press, 1899.

28 Medlicott, W. N. *Bismarck and Modern Germany*, Athlone Press, 1965.

29 Palmer, A. *Bismarck*, Charles Scribner's Sons, 1976.

30 Pflanze, O. *Bismarck and the Development of Germany. The period of Unification, 1815–71*, Princeton University Press, 1963.

31 Snyder, L. L. *The Blood and Iron Chancellor. A Documentary Biography of Otto von Bismarck*, D. Van Nostrand Co. Inc., 1967.

32 Taylor, A. J. P. *Bismarck. The Man and the Statesman*, Hamish Hamilton, 1955.

BACKGROUND HISTORY
33 Carr, W. *A History of Germany, 1815–1945*, Edward Arnold, 1969.
34 Craig, G. A. *Germany 1866–1945*, Oxford University Press, 1978.
35 Dawson, W. H. *The German Empire, 1867–1914 and the Unity Movement*, 2 vols, Allen and Unwin, 1919.
36 Grenville, J. A. S. *Europe Reshaped, 1848–1876*, Fontana/Collins, 1976.
37 Hamerow, T. *Restoration, Revolution, Reaction. Economics and Politics in Germany, 1815–1871*, Princeton University Press, 1958.
38 Holborn, H. *A History of Modern Germany, 1840–1945*, Eyre & Spottiswoode, 1969.
39 Koch, H. W. *A History of Prussia*, Longman, 1978.
40 Mann, G. *The History of Germany since 1789*, Chatto and Windus, 1968.
41 Passant, E. J. *A Short History of Germany, 1815–1945*, Cambridge University Press, 1962
42 Pinson, K. *Modern Germany – Its History and Civilization*, Macmillan (New York), 1954.
43 Ramm, A. *Germany, 1789–1919. A Political History*, Methuen, 1967.
44 Rosenberg, A. *Imperial Germany. The birth of the German Republic, 1871 – 1918*, Oxford University Press, 1970.
45 Sheehan, J. J. 'Leadership in the German Reichstag, 1871–1918', *American Historical Review*, 54, 1966.
46 Stone, N. *Europe Transformed, 1878–1919*, Fontana, 1983.
47 Stürmer, M. *Das Ruhelose Reich – Deutschland, 1866–1918*, Severin and Siedler, 1983.
48 Taylor, A. J. P. *The Course of German History*, Methuen, 1961.
49 Wehler, H-U. *Das deutsche Kaiserreich, 1871–1918*, Vandenhoeck und Ruprecht, 1973. (Translated as *The German Empire*, Berg, 1984.)

POLITICAL AND CONSTITUTIONAL HISTORY, 1862–90
50 Anderson, M. L. *Windthorst. A Political Biography*, Oxford University Press, 1981.

51 Belli, J. and Schütz, H. J. (eds.) *Die Rote feldpost unterem Sozialistengesetz*, Dietz Nachf GmbH, 1978.

52 Berdahl, R. M. 'Conservative Politics and Aristocratic Landholders in Bismarckian Germany', *Journal of Modern History*, 44, 1972.

53 Bos, T. K. 'Die Verhandlung über den Eintritt der Süddeutschen Staaten in den Norddeutschen Bund und die Entstehung der Reichverfassung', in Schieder, T. and Deuerlein, E. (eds.) *Reichsgründung 1870–71, Tatsachen, Kontroversen, Interpretation*, Seewald Verlag, 1970.

54 Huber, E. R. *Deutsche Verfassungsgeschichte seit 1789*, vols 3 and 4, Kohlhammer, 1963 and 1969.

55 Kolb, E. 'Kriegführung and Politik, 1870–71' in Schieder, T. and Deuerlein, E. (eds.) *Reichsgründung 1871*, Seewald Verlag, 1970.

56 Lidtke, V. L. *The Outlawed Party – Social Democracy in Germany, 1878–1890*, Princeton University Press, 1966.

57 Mitchell, A. 'Bonapartism as a Model for Bismarckian Politics', *Journal of Modern History*, 49(2), 1977.

58 Mork, G. R. 'Bismarck and the Capitulation of German Liberalism', *Journal of Modern History*, 43(1), 1971.

59 Rich, N. *Friedrich von Holstein: Politics and Diplomacy in the Era of Bismarck and Wilhelm II*, 2 vols, Cambridge University Press, 1965.

60 Röhl, J. C. G. 'The Disintegration of the Kartell and the Politics of Bismarck's fall from Power, 1887–90' *Historical Journal*, 9, 1966.

61 Sheehan, J. J. *German Liberalism in the Nineteenth Century*, Methuen, 1982.

62 Snyder, L. L. 'Bismarck and the Lasker Resolution, 1884', *Review of Politics*, 29(1), 1967.

63 Stürmer, M. 'Staatsstreichgedanken im Bismarckreich', *Historische Zeitschrift*, 209, 1969.

64 Stürmer, M. *Regierung und Reichstag im Bismarckstaat, 1871–1880: Cäsarismius oder Parlamentarismus*, Droste, 1974.

65 Van der Kiste, J. *Frederick III – German Emperor, 1888*, Alan Sutton, 1981.

66 Winckler, H. 'Preussischer Liberalismus und Deutscher Nationalstaat' in Möhr, J. C. B. *Studien zur Geschichte der Deutschen Fortschrittspartei, 1861–1866*, Paul Siebeck, 1964.

67 Windell, G. G. 'Bismarckian Empire: Chronicle of Failure, 1866–1880' in *Central European History*, 2(4), 1969.

ECONOMIC AND SOCIAL HISTORY

68 Anderson, E. N. *The Social and Political Conflict in Prussia, 1858–1864*, University of Nebraska, 1954.

69 Barkin, A. 'A Wagner and German Industrial Development', *Journal of Modern History*, 41, 1969.

70 Blanke, R. 'Bismarck and the Prussian Polish Policies of 1886', *Journal of Modern History*, 45, 1973.

71 Boehme, H. *Deutschlands Weg zur Grossmacht*, Kiepenhauer and Witsch, 1966.

72 Clapham, J. H. *Economic Development of France and Germany, 1815–1914*, Cambridge University Press, 1921.

73 Evans, R. J. (ed.) *Society and Politics in Wilhelmine Germany*, Croom Helm, 1978.

74 Farr, I. 'From Anti-Catholicism to Anticlericalism: Catholic Politics and the Peasantry in Bavaria, 1860–1900', *European Studies Review*, 13, 1983.

75 Hales, E. E. Y. *The Catholic Church in the Modern World*, Eyre and Spottiswoode, 1958.

76 Hamerow, T. *The Social Foundations of German Unification*, vol 1, 'Ideas and Institutions', Princeton University Press, 1969, vol 2, 'Struggles and Accomplishments', Princeton University Press, 1972.

77 Henderson, W. O. *The Zollverein*, (new impression), Cass, 1968.

78 Kardorff, S. von, *Wilhelm von Kardorff*, Mittler and Sohn, 1936.

79 Kehr, E. *Economic Interest, Militarism and Foreign Policy*, (trans. and ed. Craig, G.), University of California Press, 1977.

80 Lambi, I. N. *Free Trade and Protection in Germany, 1868–1879*, Steiner, 1963.

81 Masur, G. *Imperial Berlin*, Routledge and Kegan Paul, 1971.

82 Milward, A. G. and Saul, S. B. *The Development of the Economies of Continental Europe, 1850–1914*, Allen and Unwin, 1977.

83 Mork, G. R. 'The Prussian Railway Scandal of 1873: Economics and Politics in the German Empire', *European Studies Review*, I(1), 1971.

84 Rosenberg, H. 'Political and Social Consequences of the Great Depression of 1873–1896 in Central Europe', *Economic History Review*, 13, 1943.

85 Rosenberg H. 'Grosse Depression und Bismarckzeit', *Veröffentlichung der Historischen Kommission zu Berlin*, 24, Walter de Gruyter, 1967.

86 Sauer, W. 'Das Problem des deutschen Nationalstaates', in Wehler, H-U (ed.) *Moderne Deutsche Sozialgeschichte*, Kiepenheuer and Witsch, 1966.

87 Silverman, D. P. 'Political Catholicism and Social Democracy in Alsace-Lorraine, 1871–1914', *Catholic Review*, 52(1), 1966.

88 Silverman, D. P. *Reluctant Union – Alsace-Lorraine and Imperial Germany, 1871–1918*, Pennsylvania State University Press, 1972.

89 Stehlin, S. 'Bismarck and the New Province of Hanover', *Canadian Journal of History*, 4(2), 1969.

90 Stehlin, S. *Bismarck and the Guelph Problem*, Martinius Nijhoff, 1973.

91 Stern, F. *The Politics of Cultural Despair – A Study in the Rise of the Germanic Ideology*, University of California Press, 1961.

92 Stern, F. 'Gold and Iron: Bleichröder and Bismarck', *American Historical Review*, 75(1), 1969.

93 Stern, F. *Gold and Iron: Bismarck, Bleichröder and the building of the German Empire*, George Allen and Unwin, 1977.

94 Zorn, W. 'Wirtschafts – und Sozialgeschichtliche Zusammenhänge der deutschen Reichsgründungszeit' in Wehler, H. (ed.) *Moderne deutsche sozialgeschichte*, Kiepenhauer und Witsch, 1966.

THE PRUSSIAN ARMY AND WAR

95 Craig, G. *The Politics of the Prussian Army, 1640–1945*, Oxford University Press, 1955.

96 Craig, G. *The Battle of Königgratz*, Weidenfeld and Nicolson, 1965.

97 Howard, M. *The Franco-Prussian War*, Rupert Hart Davis, 1962.

98 Howard, M. 'William I and the Reform of the Prussian Army', in Gilbert, M. (ed.) *A Century of Conflict: Essays for A. J. P. Taylor*, Hamish Hamilton, 1966.

99 Ritter, G. 'The Sword and the Sceptre', *The Prussian Tradition, 1740–1890*, vol 1, University of Miami Press, 1969.

FOREIGN POLICY

100 Anderson, M. S. *The Eastern Question 1774–1923*, Macmillan, 1966.

101 Becker, O. 'Der Sinn der Dualistischen Verständigungsversuche Bismarcks vor dem Kriege 1866', *Historische Zeitschrift*, 169, 1949.

102 Carroll, E. M. *Germany and the Great Powers, 1866–1914*, Prentice Hall, 1938.

103 Cecil, L. *The German Diplomatic Service, 1871–1914*, Princeton University Press, 1976.

104 Clark, C. W. 'Bismarck, Russia and the War of 1870', *Journal of Modern History*, 14(2), 1942.

105 Craig, G. *From Bismarck to Adenauer: Aspects of German Statecraft*, Johns Hopkins Press, 1958.

106 Dittrich, J. 'Ursachen und Ausbruch des deutschfranzösischen Krieges, 1870–71', in Schieder, T. and Deuerlein, E. (eds.) *Reichsgründung, 1870–71*, Seewald Verlag, 1970.

107 Friedjung, H. *The Struggle for Supremacy in Germany 1859–1866*, Macmillan, 1935.

108 Gall, L. 'Das Problem Elsass-Lothringen' in Schieder, T. and Deuerlein, E. (eds.) *Reichsgründung, 1870–71*, Seewald Verlag, 1970.

109 Geiss, I. *German Foreign Policy, 1871–1914*, Routledge, 1976.

110 Geuss, H. *Bismarck und Napoleon III; Ein Beitrag zur Geschichte der Preussisch-Französischen Beziehungen, 1851–1871*, Böhlau, 1959.

111 Halperin, S. W. 'The Origins of the Franco-Prussian War Revisited: Bismarck and the Hohenzollern Candidature for the Spanish Throne', *Journal of Modern History*, 45(1), 1973.

112 Kennan, G. F. *The Decline of Bismarck's European Order*, Princeton University Press, 1979.

113 Kolb, E. *Der Kriegsausbruch 1870: Politische Entscheidungsprozesse und Verantwortlichkeiten in der Julikrise 1870*, Vandenhoeck und Ruprecht, 1970.

114 Kraehe, E. 'Austria and the Problem of Reform in the German Confederation, 1815–1863', *American Historical Review*, 56, 1951.

115 Langer, W. L. *European Alliances and Alignments, 1871–1890*, Alfred A. Knoff, 1931

116 Lippgens, W. 'Bismarck, die öffentliche Meinung und die Annexion von Elsass und Lothringen', *Historische Zeitschrift*, 199, 1964.

117 Lord, R. H. *The Origins of the War of 1870*, Harvard University Press, 1924.

118 Medlicott, W. N. *The Congress of Berlin and After*, Methuen, 1938.

119 Medlicott, W. N. 'Bismarck and the Three Emperors' Alliance, 1881–87', *Transactions Roy. Hist. Soc.*, 27, 1945.

120 Medlicott, W. N. *Bismarck, Gladstone and the Concert of Europe*, Athlone Press, 1956.

121 Mosse, W. E. *The European Powers and the German Question, 1848–71*, Cambridge University Press, 1958.

122 Müller-Link, H. *Industrialisierung und Aussenpolitik Preussen-Deutschlands und das Zarenreich von 1860–1890*, Vandenhoeck und Ruprecht, 1977.

123 Röhl, J. C. G. 'Kriegsgefahr und Gasteiner Konvention – Bismarck, Eulenburg und die Vertagung des preussisch – österreichischen Krieges im Sommer 1865', in Geiss, I. and Wendt, B. J. (eds.) *Deutschland in der Weltpolitik des 19 and 20 Jahrhunderts*, Bettelsmann Universitätsverlag, 1973.

124 Steefel, L. D. 'The Schleswig-Holstein Question', *Harvard Historical Studies*, 32, Harvard University Press, 1932.

125 Steefel, L. D. *Bismarck, the Hohenzollern Candidacy and the Origins of the Franco-German War of 1870*, Harvard University Press, 1962.

126 Taylor, A. J. P. *The Struggle for Mastery in Europe, 1848–1918*, Oxford University Press, 1954.

127 Taylor, A. J. P. *Habsburg Monarchy, 1815–1918*, Hamish Hamilton, 1948.

128 Waller, B. *Bismarck at the Crossroads, the Restoration of German Foreign Policy after the Congress of Berlin*, Athlone Press, 1974.

COLONIAL POLICY

129 Bley, H. *S.W. Africa under German Rule, 1894–1914*, Northwestern University Press, 1971.

130 Gann, L. H. and Duignan, P. *The Rulers of German Africa*, Stanford University Press, 1977.

131 Iliffe, J. *Tanganyika under German Rule*, Cambridge University Press, 1969.

132 Jacobs, M. G. 'Bismarck and the Annexation of New Guinea', *Historical Studies: Australia and New Zealand*, 5, 1951.

133 Kennedy, P. M. 'German Colonial Expansion: Has the 'Manipulated Social Imperialism' been antedated?' *Past and Present*, 54, 1972.

134 Kennedy, P. M. 'Bismarck's Imperialism: The Case of Samoa, 1880–1890', *Historical Journal*, 15, 1972.

135 Smith W. D. *The German Colonial Empire*, University of North Carolina Press, 1978.

136 Strandmann, H. Pogge von, 'The Domestic Origins of

Germany's Colonial Expansion under Bismarck', *Past and Present*, 42, 1969.

137   Taylor, A. J. P. *Germany's First Bid for Colonies, 1884–1885*, Macmillan, 1938.

138   Townsend, M. E. *The Rise and Fall of Germany's Colonial Empire*, Macmillan (New York), 1930.

139   Turner, H. A. 'Bismarck's Imperialist Venture: Anti-British in Origin?' in Gifford, P., Louis, W. R. and Smith, A. (eds.) *Britain and Germany in Africa: Imperial Rivalry and Colonial Rule*, Yale University Press, 1967.

140   Wehler, H-U. *Bismarck und der Imperialismus*, Kiepenheuer and Witsch, 1969.

141   Wehler, H-U. 'Bismarck's Imperialism, 1862–1890', *Past and Present*, 48, 1970.

BISMARCK'S LEGACY

142   Balfour, M. *The Kaiser and His Times*, Cresset Press, 1964.

143   Berghahn, V. R. *Germany and the Approach of War in 1914*, Macmillan, 1973.

144   Epstein, K. 'Gerhard Ritter and the First World War', in Koch, H. W. (ed.) *The Origins of the First World War*, Macmillan, 1972.

145   Fischer, F. *Germany's Aims in the First World War*, Chatto and Windus, 1967.

146   Meinecke, F. *The German Catastrophe*, (trans.), Harvard University Press, 1950.

147   Nichols, J. A. *Germany After Bismarck, the Caprivi Era*, Harvard University Press, 1958.

148   Röhl, J. C. G. *Germany without Bismarck. The Crisis of Government in the Second Reich, 1890–1900*, Batsford, 1967.

THE BISMARCK DEBATE

149   Dorpalen, A. 'The German Historians and Bismarck', *Review of Politics*, 15, 1953.

150   Gall, L. (ed.) *Das Bismarck – Problem in der Geschichtsschreibung nach 1945*, Kiepenhauer and Witsch, 1971.

151   Gooch, G. P. 'The Study of Bismarck', in *Studies in German History*, Longman, 1948.

152   Kehr, E. 'Modern German Historiography', in *Economic Interest, Militarism and Foreign Policy*, (trans. and ed. Craig, G.), University of California Press, 1977.

153 Kohn, H. 'Rethinking Recent German History', *Review of Politics*, 14, 1952.

154 Kohn, H. (ed.) *German History: Some New German Views*, Allen and Unwin, 1954.

155 Pflanze, O. 'Bismarck and German Nationalism', *American Historical Review*, 60, 1955.

156 Ritter, G. 'The Last Great Cabinet Statesman', in Hamerow, T. (ed.) *Otto von Bismarck. A Historical Assessment*, D. C. Heath and Co, 1972.

157 Schmitt, H. A. 'Bismarck as Seen From the Nearest Church Steeple: A Comment on Michael Stürmer', *Central European History*, 6(4), 1973.

158 Steefel, L. D. 'Bismarck', *Journal of Modern History*, 2, 1930.

159 Stürmer, M. 'Bismarck in Perspective', *Central European History*, 4, 1971.

Index

135

Index

Constitutional crisis (1862–6), 3–4, 9–14, 25
Crankshaw, E., 19
Crash of 1873, 45, 48, 53
Cretan revolt, 31
Crimean alliance, 38
Cyprus, 68

Danish Nationalists, 29, 52, 109–12
Delbrück, R., 43, 54
Denmark, 17–19
Depression, Great, 45–9, 53, 68, 82
Deputy bill, 44, 55
Derby, Lord, 77
Disraeli, B., 65, 70
Discretionary relief bill, 58
Dual Alliance, 70, 73, 119–20

East Elbian depopulation, 46, 104
Eastern question, 31, 66–8, 72–4
Egypt, 72, 78–9
Elections, British, 70; French, 72; Prussian, 4, 11, 13–14, 25, 44, 57; N. German Confederation, 29, 97; *Reich*, 44, 48, 52, 58, 60–1, 63, 76, 109–12; *Zollverein*, 34
Ems Telegram, 37, 99
Eugenie, Empress of France, 38, 41
Eyck, E., 5, 37

Falk, A., 52
Ferry, J., 72
Fiji Isles, 77, 123
Fischer, F., 5
Fontane, T., 64
France (also French), Second Empire, 2, 8, 12, 15–17, 20, 23–4, 31–3, 36–8, 90, 97–9; Govt. of Nat. Defence, 39, 41; Third Republic, 65–6, 70–5, 78, 83
Frankfurt, 24, 26; Diet, 7, 16, 21–2, 27, 85, 89, 93–4; Parliament (1848), 17, 91; Peace of, 41, 65
Franz Joseph, Emperor, 20, 21, 23–4, 38, 66
Frederick III (also Crown Prince), 26, 61–2, 76
Frederick VII, 17
Free Conservatives, 25, 29, 61, 109–12
Free Trade, 2, 12, 15–16, 47, 53, 56; Treaty, 20

Gablenz brothers, 22
Galicia, 38
General German Workers Union, 11, 48
German Empire (Reich), foundation, 2, 40–1; 'second foundation', 57; constitution, 40–1, 82; and Prussia, 43–4; finances, 53–6; post Bismarck, 82–3
German colonial Empire, 76–80
German 'Gladstone ministry', 76
German 'revolution', 65
Giers, N., 71
Gilchrist-Thomas Process, 46
Goltz, R.v. der, 23, 93
Gorchakov, A., 37, 67
Gramont, A., 37
Granville, Lord, 77
Grossdeutsch, 17, 81
Gründerjahre, 45
Gold Coast, 78
Guelphs, 26, 29, 109–12
Guizot, F., 82

Hagen proposal, 4
Hamburg, 1, 23, 77, 85
Hanover, 24, 26, 85
Hansemann, A.v., 12
Health insurance, 60
Heidelberg declaration, 58
Helldorf-Bedra, O.v., 64
Hesse-Darmstadt, 24; Kassel, 24, 26; south, 33
Heydt, A.v. der, 4
Hitler, A., 5
Hohenlohe, Prince, 34, 82
Holland, King of, 32; Queen of, 118–19
Holstein, *see* Schleswig-Holstein
Holstein, F.v., 63, 74
Holy Alliance, 16, 66

Imperialism, 76–80, see also social imperialism
Indemnity bill, 25
Industrial revolution 48, 103
'Iron' budget, 29, 32, 35
'Is war in sight' crisis, 66
Isabella, Queen, 36
Italy, 2, 12, 22, 38, 51, 71, 73–4, 86

Index

Protectionism, 47–8, 53–6, 58, 105–6
Prussia, 1–3, 7–8, 15–24, 26–8, 31–4, 40–1, 43–4, 82, 85, 87, 89, 91–4, 96
Prussian Council on Political Economy, 59; Cabinet, 4, 43, 59; Civil Service, 10, 59, 117; *Landtag*, 3–4, 9–14, 21, 25–6, 44, 52, 86, 89; United Diet, 7

Radowitz plan, 3, 7
Railways, 1, 21, 35, 45, 47, 54, 94
Rechberg, J.v., 20
Reich Chancellor's office, 43
Reichstag, Constituent, 28–30, 32–3, 97; N. German Confederation, 35, 41; German, 44, 52, 54–61, 63–4, 81–2, 109–12, 117–18
Reinsurance Treaty, 73–4
Revolt of 1848, 1, 2, 5, 17, 23
Rhineland, 23–4, 52
Richter, E., 53
Ritter, G., 12
Rome, 28, 51
Roon, A.v., 3, 8–10, 13, 93, 101
Ruhr coal strike, 62
Rumania, 71
Russia, 8, 10, 15–17, 38–9, 47, 54, 65–75, 79, 83, 96, 119–122

Saburov, P., 70
Sadowa, see Königgratz
Samoa, 80
Sammlung, 6, 57, 60–1
Savoy, 15
Saxony, 24, 54
Schleswig-Holstein, 13, 17–22, 82, 92–5
Schönbrunn conference, 20
Schwarzenberg, Prince, 7
Sedan, 38–40, 52
Septennat, 50, 61
Serbia, 67, 71
Sheehan, J., 5
Silesia, 1, 20
Skobelev, General, 71
Social imperialism, 6, 76
Social Democratic Party (*SPD*), 48, 58–62, 82, 109–12, 120

South Seas, 77
Stern, F., 9, 21
Stoecker, A., 58
Straits, the, 70, 73
Strasburg, 72
Strousberg, B. H., 45
Stürmer, M., 5, 6
Syllabus Errorum, 51

Tariffs, 47–8, 54–7, 61, 68–9, 71, 81–2, 106, 116, *see also* protectionism
Taylor, A. J. P., 31, 50, 72, 76, 78
Three Emperors Alliance, 70–3, 120
Third *Reich*, 5, 6
Trade unions, 58
Triple Alliance, 71, 74
Togoland, 79
Tunis, 71–2
Turkish Empire, 66–8

Uganda, 80
Universal (male) franchise, 11, 23, 28, 44, 114

Versen, M., v., 37
Venetia, 15, 19, 20, 22–4
Vienna settlement, 1, 7, 17, 90

Waldersee, v., Field-Marshal, 62, 74
War, Austro-Prussian, 13, 16, 19–24; Crimean, 1, 8, 15; Danish (1864), 11, 13, 18–19, 91; Franco-Prussian, 37–42, 65, 100; Russo-Turkish, 67
Wehler, H-U., 5, 76, 87
William I., Regent, King and Emperor, 3, 4, 8–11, 13, 16–17, 20–1, 23, 27, 35, 37, 41, 43–4, 55, 69–70, 86–7, 95, 99
William II, Emperor, 62–4, 74, 82, 117
Windthorst, L., 51–2, 56, 58, 63, 113
Wrangel, F.v., 18
Württemberg, 20, 24, 34–5, 40–1, 54, 90

Zanzibar, 79, 80
Zedlitz, C.v., 20
Zentrum, 50–63, 109–12, 116–17
Zollverein, 1–2, 8, 12, 15–17, 20–1, 24, 33, 40; parliament, 33–4